debbie bliss
THE CELTIC COLLECTION

D0490850

debbie bliss
THE CELTIC COLLECTION

Over 25 designs for babies, children and adults

EBURY PRESS
LONDON

To Barry, Billy and Nell

First published in Great Britain in 2000

1 3 5 7 9 10 8 6 4 2

Text and knitwear designs © Debbie Bliss, 2000
Photographs © Craig Fordham, 2000

Debbie Bliss has asserted her right to be identified as the author of this work under the Copyright, Designs and Patents Act 1988.

The knitwear designs in this book are copyright and must not be knitted for resale.

All rights reserved. No part of this publication may be reproduced, stored in a retrieval system, or transmitted in any form or by any means, electronic, mechanical, photocopying, recording or otherwise without the prior permission of the copyright owners.

First published by Ebury Press, Random House,
20 Vauxhall Bridge Road, London SW1V 2SA

Random House Australia (Pty) Limited
20 Alfred Street, Milsons Point, Sydney, New South Wales 2061, Australia

Random House New Zealand Limited
18 Poland Road, Glenfield, Auckland 10, New Zealand

Random House South Africa (Pty) Limited
Endulini, 5A Jubilee Road, Parktown 2193, South Africa

The Random House Group Limited Reg. No. 954009

www.randomhouse.co.uk

A CIP catalogue record for this book is available from the British Library.

Editor: Emma Callery
Designer: Christine Wood
Photographer: Craig Fordham
Stylist: Jemima Mills

ISBN 0 09186947 1

Papers used by Ebury Press are natural, recyclable products made from wood grown in sustainable forests.

Printed and bound in Italy by New Interlitho S.p.a

THE CITY OF EDINBURGH COUNCIL	
C0016645987	
Morley Books	4.5.00
TT820	£12.99
RA	LE2

contents

Introduction

Inspired by the legends and landscapes of the Celts, my latest collection of designs ranges from simple knits in speckled tweeds to delicate shaded Fair Isles and intricate, cabled Arans. There are also designs to cover knitting skills from easy to advanced and for a range of ages from babies to adults.

This book has given me the opportunity to share my love of the traditional stitch patterns of Ireland and mainland Britain. Inspired by their colour and texture, I have given my designs a more contemporary look by introducing subtle shaping to cabled jackets or contrast edgings to enhance classic styles.

I have chosen yarns that reflect the textures and hues of the countryside: chunky tweeds for dry stone walls, creams and chocolate browns for the dark, cool interiors of a Welsh farmhouse, and faded blues and greys with lilacs for misty, washed-out skies and heathered moors. The end result is a book that has given me enormous pleasure to create and one that I hope will inspire you to make at least one or two of the garments contained within these pages.

Debbie Bliss

Basic information

Notes

Figures for larger sizes are given in round ( ) brackets. Where only one figure appears, this applies to all sizes. Work figures given in square [ ] brackets the number of times stated afterwards. Where 0 appears, no stitches or rows are worked for this size.

The yarn amounts given in the instructions are based on average requirements and should therefore be considered approximate. If you want to use a substitute yarn, choose a yarn of the same type and weight as the one recommended.

The amount of a substitute yarn needed is determined by the number of metres/yards needed rather than by the number of grams/ounces. If you are unsure when choosing a substitute, ask your yarn shop to advise you.

Tension

Each pattern in this book specifies a tension - the number of stitches and rows per centimetre/inch that should be obtained with the given needles, yarn and stitch pattern. Check your tension carefully before commencing work.

Use the same yarn, needles and stitch pattern as those to be used for the main work and knit a sample at least 12.5cm/5in square. Smooth out the finished sample on a flat surface, but do not stretch it. To check the tension, place a rule horizontally on the sample and mark 10cm/4in across with pins. Count the number of stitches between the pins. To check the row tension, place a ruler vertically on the sample and mark 10cm/4in with pins. Count the number of rows between the pins. If the number of stitches and rows is greater than specified, try again using larger needles; if less, use smaller needles. The stitch tension is the most important element to get right.

Knitting terms

A few specific knitting or crochet terms may be unfamiliar to some readers. The list below explains the abbreviations used in this book to help the reader understand how to follow the various stitches and stages.

Standard abbreviations

alt = alternate

beg = begin(ning)

cont = continue

dec = decreas(e)ing

foll = following

gst = garter stitch

inc = increas(e)ing by working into front and back of stitch

k = knit

m1 = make one by picking up the loop lying just between st just worked and next st and working into the back of it

mst = moss stitch

patt = pattern

p = purl

psso = pass slipped stitch over

rem = remaining

rep = repeat

skpo = slip 1, knit 1, pass slipped stitch over

sl = slip

st(s) = stitch(es)

st st = stocking stitch

tbl = through back of loop

tog = together

yb = yarn back

yf = yarn forward

yon = yarn over needle

yrn = yarn round needle

Important

Check on ball band for washing instructions. After washing, pat garments into shape and dry flat, away from direct heat.

Rowan Denim will shrink and fade when it is washed, just like a pair of jeans. Unlike many 'denim look' yarns, this one uses real indigo dye, which only coats the surface of the yarn, leaving a white core that is gradually exposed through washing and wearing.

When washed for the first time, the yarn will shrink by up to one-fifth on length; the width, however, will remain the same. All the necessary adjustments have been made in the instructions for the patterns specially designed for Denim.

The knitted pieces should be washed separately at a temperature of 60-70° C (140-158° F) before you sew the garment together. The pieces can then be tumble-dried. Dye loss will be greatest during the initial wash; the appearance of the garment will, however, be greatly enhanced with additional washing and wearing. The cream denim yarn will shrink in the same way but will not fade.

The following terms may be unfamiliar to US readers

UK terms	US terms
Aran wool	'fisherman' (unbleached wool) yarn
ball band	yarn wrapper
cast off	bind off
DK wool	knitting worsted yarn
double crochet stitch	single crochet stitch
make up (garment)	finish (garment)
rib	ribbing
stocking stitch	stockinette stitch
tension	gauge

Fair Isle Cardigan with Chenille Edging

MATERIALS

4(5) 50g balls of Rowan True 4 ply Botany in Beige (M).
1(2) balls of the same yarn in each of Dark Brown, Dark Blue, Light Blue, Cream and Red.
1 ball of the same yarn in each of Green and Lilac.
1 x 50g ball of Rowan Fine Cotton Chenille in Light Blue.
Pair each of 2¾mm (No 12/US 2) and 3¼mm (No10/US 3) knitting needles.
8 buttons.

MEASUREMENTS

To fit bust sizes	81-86	91cm
	32-34	36in
Actual measurement	93.5	100.5cm
	36¾	39½in
Length	50	52.5cm
	19¾	20¾in
Sleeve seam	42	42cm
	16½	16½in

TENSION

31 sts and 35 rows, to 10cm/4in square over patt on 3¼mm (No 10/US 3) needles.

ABBREVIATIONS

See page 7.

NOTE

Read chart from right to left on right side (K) rows and from left to right on wrong side (P) rows. When working pattern, strand yarn not in use loosely across back of work to keep fabric elastic.

BACK

With 3¼mm (No 10/US 3) needles and Chenille, cast on 116(129) sts.
Change to 2¾mm (No 12/US 2) needles.
K5 rows.
Change to 3¼mm (No10/US 3) needles.
Inc row: Join in M, with M, k2(3), m1, [k4, m1] to last 2 sts, k2. 145(161) sts.
Beg with a p row and the 2nd row, work in st st and patt from chart for 34 rows, **at the same time**, dec 1 st each end of the 4th of these rows and the 5 foll 6th rows. 133(149) sts.
Patt a further 21 rows straight.
Patt 41 rows, inc 1 st at each end of the first of these rows and the 4 foll 10th rows. 143(159) sts.
Patt 11 rows straight.

Shape armholes

Cont in patt to match chart and dec 1 st at each end of the next row and the 5(7) foll alt rows. 131(143) sts.
Patt 45(49) rows straight.

Shape shoulders

Cast off 14(16) sts at beg of next 4 rows and 15(16) sts on foll 2 rows.
Cast off rem 45(47) sts.

1st size right front
1st size left front
40
30
20
10
1
1st and 2nd sizes back and sleeves
16 st rep
1st and 2nd sizes back and sleeves
2nd size right and left front
2nd size right and left front

Key
Dark Brown — Light Blue
Lilac — Dark Blue
Cream — Green
Red — M (Beige)

LEFT FRONT

With 3¼mm (No 10/US 3) needles and Chenille, cast on 59(65) sts.
Change to 2¾mm (No 12/US 2) needles.
K5 rows.
Change to 3¼mm (No 10/US 3) needles. **
Inc row: Join in M, with M, k4(2), m1, [k4, m1] to last 3 sts, k3.
73(81) sts.
*** Beg with a p row and the 2nd row, work in st st and patt from chart for 34 rows, at the same time, dec 1 st at side edge on the 4th of these rows and the 5 foll 6th rows. 67(75) sts.
Patt a further 21 rows straight.
Patt 41 rows, inc 1 st at side edge on the first of these rows and the 4 foll 10th rows. 72(80) sts.
Patt 11 rows straight.

Shape armhole

Dec 1 st at side edge on the next row and the 5(7) foll alt rows. 66(72) sts.
Patt 16(20) rows straight. Patt 17(21) rows here when working right front.

Shape neck

Next row: [Patt 3, work 2tog] twice, patt 0(1) and leave these 8(9) sts on a safety-pin, patt to end.
Dec 1 st at neck edge on next row and the 12 foll alt rows. 43(48) sts.
Patt 3 rows.

Shape shoulder

Cast off 14(16) sts at beg of next and foll alt row. 15(16) sts.
Patt 1 row.
Cast off rem 15(16) sts.

RIGHT FRONT

Work as left front to **.
Inc row: Join in M, with M k3, m1, [k4, m1] to last 4(2) sts, k4(2).
73(81) sts.
Work as left front from *** to end, noting variation.

SLEEVES

With 3¼mm (No 10/US 3) needles and Chenille, cast on 52(65) sts.
Change to 2¾mm (No 12/US 2) needles.
K5 rows.
Change to 3¼mm (No 10/US 3) needles.
Inc row: Join in M, with M, k2(3), m1, [k4, m1] to last 2 sts, k2.
65(81) sts.

Beg with a p row and the 2nd row, work 5 rows in st st and patt as given on chart.
Keeping continuity of patt, taking extra sts into patt as they occur, inc 1 st each end of the next row and the 16 foll 8th rows. 99(115) sts.
Patt a further 7 rows straight.

Shape top

Dec 1 st each end of next row and the 5(7) foll alt rows.
87(99) sts.
Patt 1 row.
Cast off.

BUTTONHOLE BAND

With right side of work facing, using 2¾mm (No 12/US 2) needles and Chenille, pick up and k94(102) sts evenly along row-ends of right front edge.
K1 row.
Buttonhole row: K3(5), yf, k2tog, [k12(13), yf, k2tog] 6 times, k5.
K1 row.
Cast off.

BUTTON BAND

With right side of work facing, using 2¾ mm (No 12/US 2) needles and Chenille, pick up and k94(102) sts evenly along row-ends of left front.
K3 rows.
Cast off.

NECKBAND

First join shoulder seams.
With right side of work facing, using 2¾mm (No 12/US 2) needles and Chenille, pick up and k3 sts from row-ends of buttonhole band, k the 8(9) sts on right front safety-pin, pick up and k22 sts up right front neck shaping, 32(34) sts across back neck, 22 sts down left front neck shaping, k the 8(9) sts on left front safety-pin, then pick up and k3 sts from row-ends of button band. 98(102) sts.
K1 row.
Buttonhole row: K2, yf, k2tog, k to end.
K1 row.
Cast off.

MAKE UP

Set sleeves into armholes. Join side and sleeve seams. Sew on buttons.

Fair Isle Scarf

MATERIALS

3 x 50g balls of Rowan True 4 ply Botany in Lilac (M).
Small amounts of the same yarn in each of Stone, Cream,
Light Blue, Dark Blue and Plum.
Small amount of Jaeger Matchmaker Merino 4 ply in Bright Pink.
1 x 50g ball of Rowan Fine Cotton Chenille in Plum.
Pair each of 2¾mm (No 12/US 2) and 3¼mm (No 10/US 3)
knitting needles.

MEASUREMENTS

Approximately 15 x 125cm/6 x 49in.

TENSION

28 sts and 36 rows to 10cm/4in square over st st on 3¼mm
(No 10/US 3) needles.

ABBREVIATIONS

See page 7.

NOTE

Read chart from right to left on right side (K) rows and from left to
right on wrong side (P) rows. When working pattern, strand yarn
not in use loosely across back of work to keep fabric elastic.

TO MAKE

With 2¾mm (No 12/US 2) needles and Chenille, cast on 83 sts.
Beg with a k row, st st 4 rows, inc 2 sts evenly across the last row.
85 sts.
Change to 3¼mm (No 10/US 3) needles and M.
Beg with a k row, st st 12 rows.
Work 13 rows from chart.
Cont in st st in M only until work measures 117cm/46in from beg,
ending with a p row.
Work 13 rows from chart.
St st 12 rows in M, dec 2 sts evenly across the last row. 83 sts.
Change to 2¾mm (No 12/US 2) needles and Chenille.
St st 4 rows.
Cast off pwise.

TO MAKE UP

Fold scarf in half lengthwise with the seam centralized. Join seam,
then join ends at cast-on and cast-off edges.

edge sts   16 st rep   edge sts

Key		
⊠	Plum	
●	Bright Pink	
·	Stone	
╱	Light Blue	
╲	Dark Blue	
─	Cream	
☐	M (Lilac)	

Simple Sweater with Collar

MATERIALS

8(9:9:10:11:12:13:14:15) 50g hanks of Rowan DK Tweed.
Pair each of 3¼mm (No 10/US 3) and
4mm (No 8/US 6) knitting needles.
A set of four 3¼mm (No 10/US 3) and 4mm (No 8/US 6) double
pointed knitting needles.

MEASUREMENTS

To fit sizes	2-4	4-6	6-8	8-9	9-10 yrs
Actual chest/bust					
measurement	82	90	94	106	110cm
	32¼	35½	37	41¾	43¼in
Length	43	48	52	56	62cm
	17	19	20½	22	24½in
Sleeve seam	28	32	36	40	44cm
with cuff turned	11	12½	14¼	15¾	17¼in
back					

To fit sizes	small	medium	large	extra large
Actual chest/bust				
measurement	122	128	132	136cm
	48	50½	52	53½in
Length	66	68	70	72cm
	26	26¾	27½	28¼in
Sleeve seam	46	48	50	52cm
with cuff turned	18	19	19¾	20½in
back				

TENSION

20 sts and 32 rows to 10cm/4in square over st st on 4mm
(No 8/US 6) needles.

ABBREVIATIONS

See page 7.

BACK

With 4mm (No 8/US 6) needles, cast on
82(90:94:106:110:122:126:130:134) sts.
1st rib row: K2, [p2, k2] to end.
2nd rib row: P2, [k2, p2] to end.
Rep the last 2 rows, for 9(9: 9:10:10:10:11:
11:11)cm/3½(3½:3½:4:4:4:4¼:4¼:4¼)in, ending with the 2nd row,
inc 1 st at each end of the last row on the 7th, 8th and 9th sizes
only. 82(90:94:106:110:122:128:132:136) sts.
Beg with a k row, work in st st until back measures
26.5(29:32:35:38.5:41:43:44:46)cm/10½(11½:12½:13¾:15:16:
17:17¼:18)in from beg, ending with a p row.
Mark each end of the last row for side seams. **
Work in st st for a further
16.5(19:20:21:23.5:25:25:26:26)cm/6½(7½:7¾:8¼:9¼:9¾:9¾:

10¼:10¼)in, ending with a p row.
Shape shoulders
Cast off 14(16:16:18:19:21:22:22:23) sts at beg of next 2 rows
and 15(16:17:19:19:22:22:23:23) sts on foll 2 rows.
Leave rem 24(26:28:32:34:36:40:42:44) sts on a st holder.

FRONT

Work as given for back to **.
Work in st st for a further 12.5(14:15:16:
17.5:19:19:19:19)cm/5(5½:6:6¼:6¾:7½:7½:7½:7½)in, ending
with a p row.
Divide for neck
Next row: K34(37:38:43:44:48:50:51:52) sts, turn and leaving
remaining sts on a spare needle, work on these sts for left half
neck.
Left half neck: P1 row, then dec 1 st at neck edge on the next row
and the 4(4:4:5:5:4:5:5:5) foll alt rows.
29(32:33:37:38:43:44:45:46) sts.
Cont in st st until front measures the same as back to shoulder
shaping, ending at side edge.
Shape shoulder
Cast off 14(16:16:18:19:21:22:22:23) sts at beg of next row.
Work 1 row.
Cast off rem 15(16:17:19:19:22:22:23:23) sts.
Right half neck: With right side facing, sl centre
14(16:18:20:22:26:28:30:32) sts on to a st holder, rejoin yarn to
inner edge of rem sts and work to end of row.
Work as given for left half neck.

SLEEVES

With 4 mm (No 8/US 6) needles, cast on
38(42:46:46:50:54:54:58:58) sts.
Work 5(5:5:6:6:6:7:7:7)cm/2(2:2:2½:2½:2½:2¾:2¾:2¾)in in rib as
given for back.
Change to 3¼mm (No 10/US 3) needles and rib a further
5(5:5:6:6:6:7:7:7)cm/2(2:2:2½:2½:2½:2¾:2¾:2¾)in.
Change to 4mm (No 8/US 6) needles.
Beg with a k row, work 4(4:4:4:2:2:2:2:2) rows in st st.
Keeping continuity of st st, inc 1 st at each end of next row and the
13(16:16:18:21:22 22:22:22) following 4th(4th:4th:4th:4th:4th:
4th:4th:6th) rows. 66(76:80:84:94:100:100:104:104) sts.
Cont in st st until sleeve measures 33(37:41:46:50:52:55:57:
59)cm/13(14½:16:18:19½:20½:21½:22½:23¼)in from beg,
ending with a p row.
Cast off.

NECKBAND AND COLLAR

Join shoulder seams. With right side facing, using the set of four
3¼mm (No 10/US 3) double pointed needles, sl the first
7(8:9:10:11:13:14:15:16) sts from centre front st holder on to a
safety-pin, k rem 7(8:9:10:11:13:14:15:16) sts, pick up and
k17(17:17:18:18:19:20:20:20) sts up right half neck, k the
24(26:28:32:34:36:40:42:44) sts from back neck st holder, pick

up and k17(17:17:18:18:19:20:20:20) sts down left half neck, then k the 7(8:9:10:11:13:14:15:16) sts from safety-pin.
72(76:80:88:92:100:108:112:116) sts.
Beg and ending at centre front, arrange sts evenly on 3 needles and using 4th needle, work in rounds as follows:
1st round : P1, [k2, p2] to last 3 sts, k2, p1.
Rep the last round for 3(3:3:
3:4:4:4:5:5)cm/1¼(1¼:1¼:1¼:1½:1½:1½:2:2)in, turn.
Working backwards and forwards in rows, cont thus:
1st row: K1, [p2, k2] to last 3 sts, p2, k1.

2nd row: P1, [k2, p2] to last 3 sts, k2, p1.
Rep last 2 rows for 4cm/1½in.
Change to 4mm (No 8/US 6) double pointed needles.
Work in rib for a further
4(4:4:4:5:5:5:5:5)cm/1½(1½:1½:1½:2:2:2:2:2)in.
Cast off loosely in rib.

TO MAKE UP
Sew cast-off edge of sleeves to row-ends above markers on back and front. Join side and sleeve seams.

Denim Tunic with Pockets

MATERIALS

6(8:10:11:13:15) 50g balls of Rowan Denim.
Pair each of 3¼mm (No 10/US 3) and 4mm (No 8/US 6) knitting needles.

MEASUREMENTS

To fit ages	6 months	1	2	3	4	5 years
Actual chest measurement	57	65	75	85	91	97cm
	22½		25½	29½	33½	36	38in
Length	28		32	37	41	45	48cm
	11		12½	14½	16¼	17¾	18¾in
Sleeve seam with	17		20	22	24	28	33cm
cuff turned back	6¾		8	8¾	9½	11	13in

TENSION BEFORE WASHING

See basic information on page 6.
20 sts and 30 rows to 10cm/4in square over mst on 4mm (No 8/US 6) needles.

ABBREVIATIONS

See page 7.

BACK

With 4mm (No 8/US 6) needles, cast on 57(65:75:85:91:97) sts.
Mst row: K1, [p1, k1] to end.
This row forms the mst. **
Cont in mst until work measures 29(34:40:45:49:53)cm/11½(13¼:15¾:17¾:19¼:20¾)in from beg, ending with a wrong side row.
*** **Divide for neck**
Next row: Patt 20(24:28:33:35:38) sts, turn and leaving rem sts on a spare needle, work on these sts for right half neck.
Right half neck: Patt 1 row.
Dec 1 st at neck edge on next row and the 3(5:7:8:8:9) foll alt rows. 16(18:20:24:26:28) sts.
Cont in mst until work measures 35(40:46:52:56:60)cm/13¾(15¾:18:20½:22:23½)in from beg, ending at side edge.
Shape shoulder
Cast off 8(9:10:12:13:14) sts at beg of next row.
Patt 1 row.
Cast off rem 8(9:10:12:13:14) sts.
Left half neck: With right side facing, sl centre 17(17:19:19:21:21) sts on to a st holder, rejoin yarn to inner edge of rem sts and mst to end of row.
Work as right half neck.

POCKET LININGS (MAKE 2)

With 4mm (No 8/US 6) needles, cast on 21(23:25:27:27:29) sts.
Work in mst for 30(32:34:36:38:40) rows.
Leave sts on a st holder.

FRONT

Work as back to **.
Cont in mst until work measures 12(14:16:18:20:22)cm/5(5½:6¼:7:8:8¾)in from beg, ending with a right side row.
1st pocket row: Mst 6(8:10:12:14:14) sts, cast off next 21(23:25:27:27:29) sts, mst a further 2(2:4:6:8:10) sts, cast off next 21(23:25:27:27:29) sts, mst to end.
2nd pocket row: Mst 6(8:10:12:14:14) sts, mst across the 21(23:25:27:27:29) sts of one pocket lining, mst 3(3:5:7:9:11) sts, mst across the 21(23:25:27:27:29) sts of other pocket lining, mst to end. 57(65:75:85:91:97) sts.
Cont in mst until work measures 29(34:40:45:49:53)cm/11½(13¼:15¾:17¾:19¼:20¾)in from beg, ending with a wrong side row.
Work as back from *** to end.

SLEEVES

With 4mm (No 8/US 6) needles, cast on 27(29:31:35:37:41) sts.
Work in mst for 5(5:6:6:7:7)cm/2(2:2¼:2¼:2¾:2¾)in.
Change to 3¼mm (No 10/US 3) needles.
Work in mst for 5(5:6:6:7:7)cm/2(2:2¼:2¼:2¾:2¾)in.
Change to 4mm (No 8/US 6) needles.
Mst 2 rows.
Keeping continuity of mst, inc 1 st each end of next row and the 11(15:17:18:21:23) foll 4th (3rd:3rd:3rd:3rd:4th) rows. 51(61:67:73:81:89) sts.
Cont in mst until work measures 26(30:34:36:42:49)cm/10¼(11¾:13½:14:16½:19¼)in from beg, ending with a wrong side row.
Cast off.

NECKBAND

Join right shoulder seam. With right side facing, using 3¼mm (No 10/US 3) needles, pick up and k8(10:10:12:12:14) sts down left half neck, mst the 17(17:19:19:21:21) sts at centre, pick up and k8(10:10:12:12:14) sts up right half neck, 7(9:9:11:11:13) sts down right half neck, mst the 17(17:19:19:21:21) sts at centre, pick up and k8(10:10:12:12:14) sts up left half neck. 65(73:77:85:89:97) sts.
Change to 4mm (No 8/US 6) needles.
Work in mst for 7(7:8:8:9:9)cm/2¾(2¾:3¼:3¼:3½:3½)in.
Cast off loosely in mst.

TO MAKE UP

First, see Basic Information on page 7. Join left shoulder seam and neckband. Mark side edges of back and front 13(15:17:18:20:22)cm/5¼(6:6¾:7:8:8¾)in down from shoulders. Sew cast-off edge of sleeves to row-ends above markers on back and front. Join side and sleeve seams, leaving a 4cm/1¼in vent at side seams and reversing seam on cuff. Sew pocket linings to wrong side.

Boxy Aran Jacket

MATERIALS
12(13) 100g balls of Jaeger Shetland.
Pair each of 4mm (No 8/US 6) and 4½mm (No 7/US 7) needles.
A cable needle.
7 buttons.

MEASUREMENTS

To fit bust sizes	81-86	91-97cm
	32-34	36-38in
Actual measurement	114	122cm
	44¾	48in
Length	43	45cm
	17	17¾in
Sleeve seam	44	45cm
	17¼	17¾in

TENSION
18 sts and 24 rows to 10cm/4in square over reverse st st, and blackberry st panel to measure 3cm/1¼in in width, panels A and C to measure 7cm/2¾in in width and panel B to measure 9cm/3½in in width on 4½mm (No 7/US 7) needles.

ABBREVIATIONS
K or P1b = K or p1 through back of st.
MB = M1 = k1, yf, k1, yf, k1 all in same stitch, turn, k5, turn, k3, k2tog, pass 2nd, 3rd & 4th sts over 1st st.
T4R = Sl next st on to cable needle and leave at back, k1b, p1, k1b, p1 from cable needle.
T4L= Sl next 3 sts on to cable needle and leave at front, p1, k1b, p1, k1b from cable needle.
T4RB = Sl next st on to cable needle and leave at back, k1b, p1, k1b, k st from cable needle.
T4LB = Sl next 3 sts on to cable needle and leave at front, k1, k1b, p1, k1b from cable needle. Also see page 7.

PATTERN PANEL A (worked over 18 sts)
1st row (right side): K1b, p1, k1b, p3, sl next 3 sts on to cable needle and leave at front, k1b, p1, k1b, then k1b, p1, k1b from cable needle, p3, k1b, p1, k1b.
2nd row: P1, k1, p1, k3, p1, k1, p2, k1, p1, k3, p1, k1, p1.
3rd row: K1b, p1, k1b, p3, k1b, p1, k1b, k1b, p1, k1b, p3. K1b, p1, k1b.
4th row: As 2nd row.
5th row: As 1st row.
6th row: As 2nd row.
7th row: K1b, p1, k1b, p2, T4R, T4L, p2, k1b, p1, k1b.
8th row: P1, k1, p1, [k2, p1, k1, p1] 3 times.
9th row: K1b, p1, k1b, [p2, k1b, p1, k1b] 3 times.
10th to 16th rows: Work the 8th and 9th rows, 3 times more, then work the 8th row again.
17th row: K1b, p1, k1b, p2, T4L, T4R, p2, k1b, p1, k1b.
18th row: P1, k1, p1, k3, p1, k1, p2, k1, p1, k3, p1, k1, p1.
These 18 rows form the patt for panel A.

PATTERN PANEL B (worked over 23 sts)
1st row (right side): P7, T4RB, k1b, T4LB, p7.
2nd row: K7, p1, [k1, p1] 4 times, k7.
3rd row: P6, T4RB, k1, k1b, k1, T4LB, p6.
4th row: K6, p1, k1, p1, [k2, p1] twice, k1, p1, k6.
5th row: P5, T4RB, k2, k1b, k2, T4LB, p5.
6th row: K5, p1, k1, p2, k2, p1, k2, p2, k1, p1, k5.
7th row: P4, T4RB, k1b, [k2, k1b] twice, T4LB, p4.
8th row: K4, p1, [k1, p1] twice, [k2, p1] twice, [k1, p1] twice, k4.
9th row: P3, T4RB, k1, k1b, [k2, k1b] twice, k1, T4LB, p3.
10th row: K3, p1, k1, p1, [k2, p1] 4 times, k1, p1, k3.
11th row: P2, T4RB, k2, [k1b, k2] 3 times, T4LB, p2.
12th row: K2, p1, k1, p1, k3, p1, [k2, p1] twice, k3, p1, k1, p1, k2.
13th row: P2, k1b, p1, k1b, k3, MB, [k2, MB] twice, k3, k1b, p1, k1b, p2.
14th row: K2, p1, k1, p1, k3, p1b, [k2, p1b] twice, k3, p1, k1, p1, k2.
15th row: P2, k1b, p1, k1b, p3, k1b, p1, [k1b] 3 times, p1, k1b, p3, k1b, p1, k1b, p2.
16th row: K8, p1, k1, p3, k1, p1, k8.
These 16 rows form the patt for panel B.

PATTERN PANEL C (worked over 18 sts)
1st row (right side): K1b, p1, k1b, p3, sl next 3 sts on to cable needle and leave at back, k1b, p1, k1b, then k1b, p1, k1b from cable needle, p3, k1b, p1, k1b.
2nd row: P1, k1, p1, k3, p1, k1, p2, k1, p1, k3, p1, k1, p1.
3rd row: K1b, p1, k1b, p3, k1b, p1, k1b, k1b, p1, k1b, p3, k1b, p1, k1b.
4th row: As 2nd row.
5th row: As 1st row.
6th row: As 2nd row.
7th row: K1b, p1, k1b, p2, T4R, T4L, p2, k1b, p1, k1b.
8th row: P1, k1, p1, [k2, p1, k1, p1] 3 times.
9th row: K1b, p1, k1b, [p2, k1b, p1, k1b] 3 times.
10th to 16th rows: Work the 8th and 9th rows, 3 times more, then work the 8th row again.
17th row: K1b, p1, k1b, p2, T4L, T4R, p2, k1b, p1, k1b.
18th row: P1, k1, p1, k3, p1, k1, p2, k1, p1, k3, p1, k1, p1.
These 18 rows form the patt for panel C

BACK
With 4mm (No 8/US 6) needles, cast on 102(110) sts.
1st row (right side): P to end.
2nd row: P1, [k1, p1, k1 all into same st, p3 tog] to last st, p1.
3rd row: P to end.
4th row: P1, [p3tog, k1, p1, k1 all into same st] to last st, p1.

Rep last 4 rows until work measures 4cm/1½in from beg, ending with the 3rd row.

Inc row: P5(9), [m1, p3] 14 times, patt 8, [p3, m1] 14 times, p5(9). 130(138) sts.

Change to 4½mm (No 7/US 7) needles.

Work in patt thus:

1st row (right side): P2(6), work across 1st row of patt panels A, B, C, for blackberry st panel, p8, work across 1st row of patt panels A, B, C, p2(6).

2nd row: K2(6), work across 2nd row of patt panels C, B, A, for blackberry st panel, [k1, p1, k1 all into same st, p3tog] twice, work across 2nd row of patt panels C, B, A, k2(6).

3rd row: P2(6), work across 3rd row of patt panels A, B, C, for blackberry st panel, p8, work across 3rd row of panels A, B, C, p2(6).

4th row: K2(6), work across 4th row of patt panels C, B, A, for blackberry st panel, [p3tog, k1, p1, k1 all into same st] twice, work across 4th row of patt panels C, B, A, k2(6).

These 4 rows form a rep of patt for the blackberry st panel and set position of panels A, B and C.

Cont in patt as set, taking extra sts into reverse st st at side edges as they occur, inc 1 st each end of the next row and the 4 foll 8th rows. 140(148) sts.

Cont in patt until work measures 20(21)cm/8(8¼)in, from beg, ending with a wrong side row.

Shape armholes

Cast off 5(7) sts at beg of next 2 rows. 130(134) sts.

Cont in patt until work measures 43(45)cm/17(17¾)in from beg, ending with a wrong side row.

Shape shoulders

Cast off 22(23) sts at beg of next 4 rows.

Cast off rem 42 sts.

POCKET LININGS (make 2)

With 4mm (No 8/US 6) needles, cast on 19 sts.

Beg with a p row, work 15 rows in reverse st st.

Inc row: K4, m1, k5, m1, k1, m1, k5, m1, k4. 23 sts.

Work the 3rd to 7th rows of panel B.

Leave sts on a st holder.

LEFT FRONT

With 4mm (No 8/US 6) needles, cast on 54(58) sts.

1st row (right side): P to end.

2nd row: P1, [k1, p1, k1 all into same st, p3tog] to last st, p1.

3rd row: P to end.

4th row: P1, [p3tog, k1, p1, k1 all into same st] to last st, p1.**

Rep the last 4 rows until work measures 4cm/1½in from beg, ending with the 3rd row.

Inc row: Patt 9 m1, inc, p2, [m1, p3] 14 times, p0(4) 70(74) sts.

Change to 4½mm (No 7/US 7) needles.

Work in patt thus:

1st row: p2(6), work across 1st row of patt panels A, B, C, for blackberry st front band, p9.

2nd row: For blackberry st front band, p1 [k1, p1, k1 all into same st, p3tog] twice, work across 2nd row of patt panels C, B, A, k2(6).

3rd row: P2(6), work across 3rd row of patt panels A, B, C, for blackberry st front band, p9.

4th row: For blackberry st front band, p1 [p3tog, k1, p1, k1 all into same st] twice, work across 4th row of patt panels C, B, A, k2(6).

*** These 4 rows form a rep of the blackberry st front band and set position of panels A, B and C.

Cont in patt as set, taking extra sts into reverse st st at side edge as they occur, inc 1 st at side edge on next row and 2 foll 8th rows. 73(77) sts.

Patt 1 row. ***

1st pocket row: Patt 23(27), cast off next 23 sts, patt to end.

2nd pocket row: Patt 27, patt across the 23 sts of one pocket lining, patt 23(27). 73(77) sts.

**** Patt a further 4 rows.

Inc 1 st at side edge as before on the next row and the foll 8th row. 75(79) sts.

Cont in patt until work measures 20(21)cm/8(8¼)in from beg, ending at side edge.

Shape armhole

Cast off 5(7) sts at beg of next row. 70(72) sts.

Cont in patt until work measures 36(38)cm/14(15)in from beg, ending at neck edge.

Shape neck

Next row: Cast off 9 sts, patt to end.

Dec 1 st at neck edge on each of the next 17 rows. 44(46) sts.

Cont in patt until work measures 43(45)cm/17(17¾)in from beg, ending at side edge.

Shape shoulder

Cast off 22(23) sts at beg of next row.

Work 1 row.

Cast off rem 22(23) sts.

RIGHT FRONT

Mark positions for buttons on left front, placing the first marker 7 rows up from cast-on edge and a further 6 markers evenly spaced with the last marker 3 rows down from neck edge.

Work as left front to **.

Work a further 2 rows.

Buttonhole row: P4, yrn, p2tog, p2, patt to end.

Cont in patt until work measures 4cm/1½in from beg, ending with the 3rd row.

Inc row: P3(7), [m1, p3] 13 times, m1, p2, inc, m1, patt 9, 70(74) sts.

Change to 4½mm (No 7/US 7) needles.

Working in patt and making a further 6 buttonholes as before to correspond with markers on left front, cont thus:

1st row: For blackberry st front band, p9, work across 1st row of patt panels A, B, C, p2(6).

2nd row: K2(6), work across 2nd row of patt panels C, B, A, for blackberry st front band, [k1, p1, k1 all into same st, p3tog] twice, p1.

3rd row: For blackberry st front band, p9, work across 3rd row of patt panels A, B, C, p2(6).

4th row: K2(6), work across 4th row of patt panels C, B, A, for blackberry st front band [p3tog, k1, p1, k1 all into same st] twice, p1.

Work as left front from *** to ***.

1st pocket row: Patt 27 sts, cast off next 23 sts, patt to end.

2nd pocket row: Patt 23(27) sts, patt across 23 sts of other pocket lining, patt 27 sts. 73(77) sts.

Work as left front from **** to end.

SLEEVES

With 4mm (No 8/US 6) needles, cast on 46(50) sts.

Work as left front to **.

Rep the last 4 rows until work measures 4cm/1½in from beg, ending with the 3rd row.

Inc row: P2(4), [m1, p3] 14 times, m1, p2(4). 61(65) sts.

Change to 4½mm (No 7/US 7) needles.

Work patt thus:

1st row: P1(3), work across 1st row of patt panels A, B, C, p1(3).

2nd row: K1(3), work across 2nd row of patt panels C, B, A, k1(3).

These 2 rows set position of patt for panels A, B and C.

Patt a further 2 rows.

Keeping cont of patt, taking extra sts into reverse st st as they occur, inc 1 st each end of next row and the 19(20) foll 4th rows. 101(107) sts.

Cont in patt until work measures 44(45)cm/17¼(17¾)in from beg, ending with a wrong side row.

Cont in patt for a further 6(8) rows.

Cast off.

COLLAR

With 4mm (No 8/US 6) needles, cast on 102 sts.

1st row (right side): P to end.

2nd row: P1, [k1, p1, k1 all into same st, p3tog] to last st, p1.

3rd row: P to end.

4th row: P1, [p3tog, k1, p1, k1 all into same st] to last st, p1.

Rep last 4 rows until work measures 4cm/1½in from beg, ending with the 4th row.

Change to 4½mm (No 7/US 7) needles.

Work in patt for a further 5cm/2in, ending with the 4th row. Cast off loosely.

TO MAKE UP

Join shoulder seams. Sew cast-off edges of sleeves to row-ends of armholes, sewing last 6(8) row-ends of sleeves to cast-off sts at underarms. Join side and sleeve seams. Catch pocket linings to wrong side. Beginning and ending at inner edge of blackberry st front band, sew cast-on edge of collar to neck edge. Sew on buttons.

Classic Fair Isle Cardigan and Socks

MATERIALS

Cardigan: 2(3:3) 50g balls of Jaeger Matchmaker 4 ply in Oatmeal (M).
1(1:2) balls of the same yarn in Cream.
1 ball of the same yarn in each of Maroon, Blue, Cerise, Yellow and Rust.
6(7:8) buttons.
Socks: 1 x 50g ball of Jaeger Matchmaker 4 ply in Oatmeal (M).
Small amounts of the same yarn in each of Cream, Maroon, Blue, Cerise, Yellow and Rust.
For either garment: pair each of 2¾mm (No 12/US 2) and 3¼mm (No 10/US 3) knitting needles.
A set of four 3¼mm (No 10/US 3) double pointed knitting needles for socks.

MEASUREMENTS

To fit ages	6-9	9-12	24 months
Actual chest	57.5	66.5	75.5cm
measurement	22½	26¼	29¾in
Length	29	36	41cm
	11½	14¼	16in
Sleeve seam	18.5	20.5	22cm
	7¼	8	8¾in
Socks	To fit foot size 13cm/5in		

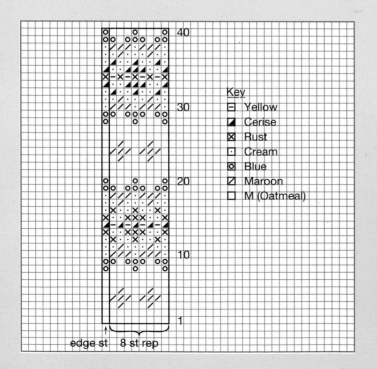

Key
⊟ Yellow
◪ Cerise
⊠ Rust
⬚ Cream
◙ Blue
◩ Maroon
☐ M (Oatmeal)

edge st   8 st rep

TENSION

35 sts and 36 rows to 10cm/4in square over patt on 3¼mm (No 10/US 3) needles.

ABBREVIATIONS

See page 7.

NOTE

Read chart from right to left on right side (K) rows and from left to right on wrong side (P) rows. When working pattern, strand yarn not in use loosely across back of work to keep fabric elastic.

CARDIGAN

BACK

With 2¾mm (No 12/US 2) needles and M, cast on 97 (113:129) sts.
1st rib row: K1, [p1, k1] to end.
2nd rib row: P1, [k1, p1] to end.
Rep last 2 rows, 3 times more.
Change to 3¼mm (No 10/US 3) needles.
Beg with a p row, work in patt from chart until 50(68:80) rows have been completed.
Mark each end of last row to denote end of side seams.
Patt a further 45(51:57) rows.

Divide for back neck

Next row: Patt 34(40:45) and leave on a spare needle for left back neck, patt 29(33:39) and leave on a st holder, patt to end and work on rem 34(40:45) sts for right back neck.

Right back neck

Dec 1 st at neck edge on each of next 4 rows. 30(36:41) sts.
Patt 1 row here when working left back neck.

Shape shoulder

Cast off 15(18:21) sts at beg of next row.
Patt 1 row.
Cast off rem 15(18:20) sts.

Left back neck

With right side facing, rejoin yarns to inner edge of 34(40:45) sts on spare needle.
Work as right back neck, noting variation.

LEFT FRONT

With 2¾mm (No 12/US 2) needles and M, cast on 49(57:65) sts.
Work 8 rows in rib as given for back.
Change to 3¼mm (No 10/US 3) needles.
Beg with a k row, work in patt from chart until 50(68:80) rows have been completed.
Mark side edge of last row to denote end of side seam.
Patt a further 33(39:45) rows.
Patt 34(40:46) rows here when working right front.

Shape neck

Next row: Patt 9(11:13) and leave on a safety-pin, patt to end.
Dec 1 st at neck edge on each of the next 10(10:11) rows.
30(36:41) sts.

Patt a further 6(6:5) rows.
Shape shoulder
Cast off 15(18:21) sts at beg of next row.
Patt 1 row.
Cast off rem 15(18:20) sts.

RIGHT FRONT
Work as left front, noting variation.

SLEEVES
With 2¾mm (No 12/US 2) needles and M, cast on 45(51:57) sts.
Work 7 rows in rib as given for back.
Inc row: Rib 3(4:6), [m1, rib 1, m1, rib 2] to last 3(5:6) sts, m1,
rib 1, m1, rib 2(4:5). 73(81:89) sts.
Change to 3¼mm (No 10/US 3) needles.
Beg with a k row, patt 2 rows from chart.
Keeping continuity of patt, taking extra sts into patt as they occur,
inc 1 st each end of the next row and the 9(11:13) foll 4th rows. 93
(105:117) sts.
Patt a further 21(19:17) rows. Cast off.

BUTTONHOLE BAND
With right side of work facing, using 2¾mm (No 12/US 2) needles
and M, pick up and k91(115:133) sts evenly along row-ends of
right front.
Beg with the 2nd row, work 2 rows in rib as given for back.
Buttonhole row: Rib 4(5:6), [work 2tog, yrn, rib 14(15:15)] 5(6:7)
times, work 2tog, yrn, rib 5(6:6).
Rib a further 3 rows.
Cast off in rib.

BUTTON BAND
With right side of work facing, using 2¾mm (No 12/US 2) needles
and M, pick up and k91(115:133) sts evenly along row-ends of left
front.
Beg with the 2nd row, work 6 rows in rib as given for back.
Cast off in rib.

COLLAR
First join shoulder seams.
With right side of work facing, using 2¾mm (No 12/US 2) needles
and M, sl 9(11:13) sts from right front safety-pin on to needle, pick
up and k18(20:22) sts up right front neck, 8 sts down right back
neck, k29(33:39) sts at back neck, pick up and k8 sts up left back
neck, 18(20:22) sts down left front neck, then k9(11:13) sts from
left front safety-pin. 99(111:125) sts.
Work 26 rows in rib as given for back.
Cast off kwise.

TO MAKE UP
Sew cast-off edge of sleeves to row-ends above markers on back
and fronts. Join side and sleeve seams. Sew on buttons.

SOCKS (make 2)

With 2¾mm (No 12/US 2) needles and M, cast on 49 sts
for cuff.

Work 4 rows in rib as given for back of cardigan.

Change to 3¼mm (No 10/US 3) needles.

Beg with a k row, work the 7th to 21st rows of chart, dec 6 sts
evenly across last row. 43 sts.

Cont with M only.

Change to 2¾mm (No 12/US 2) needles.

Beg with the 1st row (thus reversing fabric) cont in rib until work
measures 12cm/4¾in from beg, ending with a 2nd row.

Change to 3¼mm (No 10/US 3) needles.

Beg with a k row, work 4 rows in st st.

Break off yarn.

With set of four 3¼mm (No 10/US 3) double pointed needles,
divide sts on to 3 needles as follows:

Sl first 9 sts on to first needle, next 12 sts on to second needle
and foll 12 sts on to 3rd needle, sl last 10 sts on to other end of
first needle.

Shape heel

With right side facing, rejoin M to the 19 sts on first needle, k9,
k2tog, k8, turn.

Beg with a p row, work 9 rows in st st.

Next row: K13, k2tog tbl, turn.

Next row: Sl 1, p7, p2tog, turn.

Next row: Sl 1, k7, k2tog tbl, turn.

Next row: Sl 1, p7, p2tog, turn.

Rep last 2 rows, twice more. 10 sts.

Break off yarn.

Re-arrange sts on 3 needles thus: sl first 5 sts of heel on to a
safety-pin, place marker here to indicate beg of round.

Rejoin M to rem sts. With first needle k5, then pick up and
k8 sts along side of heel, k5, with second needle k14, with
3rd needle k5, then pick up and k8 sts along other side of heel,
finally, k5 from safety-pin. 50 sts.

K1 round.

Next round: K12, k2tog, k to last 14 sts,
k2tog tbl, k12.

K1 round.

Next round: K11, k2tog, k to last 13 sts,
k2tog tbl, k11.

K1 round.

Cont in this way dec 1 st each side of heel on next and 2 foll alt
rounds. 40 sts.

Cont without further shaping until work measures 11cm/4¼in from
back of heel.

Shape toe

Next round: [K7, k2tog, k2, k2tog tbl, k7] twice.

K1 round.

Next round: [K6, k2tog, k2, k2tog tbl, k6] twice.

K1 round.

Cont in this way dec 4 sts on the next round and the 2 foll alt
rounds. 20 sts.

Divide sts on to 2 needles for sole and instep and graft sts tog.
Join back seam, reversing seam for cuff edge to allow for fold
back. Fold back cuff.

Smock Jacket

MATERIALS

6(7:7) 50g balls of Jaeger Extra Fine Merino in main colour (M).
1 ball of the same yarn in a contrasting shade for embroidery.
Pair each of 3¼mm (No 10/US 3) and 3¾mm (No 9 /US 4) knitting
needles.
A cable needle.
5(6:6) buttons.

MEASUREMENTS

To fit ages	1	2	3 years
Actual chest measurement	68.5	72.5	77cm
	27	28½	30¼in
Length	39	43	48cm
	15½	17	19in
Sleeve seam	23	25	27cm
	9	9¾	10½in

TENSION

23 sts and 31 rows to 10cm/4in square over st st on 3¾mm
(No 9/US 4) needles.

ABBREVIATIONS

C2B = Sl next st on to cable needle and leave at back, k1, then
k st from cable needle.
C2F = Sl next st on to cable needle and leave at front, k1, then
k st from cable needle.
Cr2L = Sl next st on to cable needle and leave at front, p1, then
k st from cable needle.
Cr2R = Sl next st on to cable needle and leave at back, k1,
then p st from cable needle.
C4F = Sl next 2 sts on to cable needle and leave at front, k2,
then k2 from cable needle.
C4B = Sl next 2 sts on to cable needle and leave at back, k2,
then k2 from cable needle.
MB = k1, p1, k1, p1, all into same st, turn, slip 2, k2 tog, pass
sl sts over, turn, and place st on right-hand needle.
T3B = Sl next st on to a cable needle and leave at back, k2,
then p st from cable needle.
T3F = Sl next 2 sts on to cable needle and leave at front, p1,
then k2 from cable needle.
Also see page 7.

BACK

With 3¾mm (No 9/US 4) needles and M, cast on 107(113:119) sts.
Mst row: K1, [p1, k1] to end.
Mst a further 5 rows, inc 1 st at centre of last row. 108(114:120) sts.
Beg with a k row, work in st st until work measures
26(28:30.5)cm/10¼(11:12)in from beg, ending with a p row.
Shape armholes
Cast off 3 sts at beg of next 2 rows.

Dec 1 st each end of next 3 rows. 96(102:108) sts.
Beg with a p row, work 2(4:6) rows in st st.
Dec row: P8(2:1), [p2tog, p7] 0(1:1) time, * p3tog, p7, p2tog, p7;
rep from * 3(3:4) times more, [p3tog] 1(1:0) time, [p7, p2tog] 0(1:0)
time, p9(3:3). 82(86:92) sts.
Work smock patt thus:
1st row: P4(6:5), C2B, [p6, C2B] to last 4(6:5) sts, p to end.
2nd row: K3(5:4), Cr2L, Cr2R, [k4, Cr2L, Cr2R] to last 3(5:4) sts, k
to end.
3rd row: P2(4:3), Cr2R, p2, Cr2L, [p2, Cr2R, p2, Cr2L] to last
2(4:3) sts, p to end.
4th row: K1(3:2), [Cr2L, k4, Cr2R] to last 1(3:2) sts, k to end.
5th row: P1(3:2), k1, p6, [C2F, p6] to last 2(4:3) sts, k1, p to end.
6th row: K1(3:2), [Cr2R, k4, Cr2L] to last 1(3:2) sts, k to end.
7th row: P2(4:3), Cr2L, p2, Cr2R, [p2, Cr2L, p2, Cr2R] to last
2(4:3) sts, p to end.
8th row: K3(5:4), Cr2R, Cr2L, [k4, Cr2R, Cr2L] to last 3(5:4) sts, k
to end.
These 8 rows form the smock patt.
Patt a further 9 rows.
Dec row: P4(6:5), [p2tog, p1, p3tog, p2, p2tog, p2, p2tog, p2]
4(4:5) times, [p2tog, p1, p3tog, p2] 1(1:0) time, p2tog, p4(6:5).
58(62:66) sts.
Beg with a k row, work 20(22:24) rows in st st.
Shape shoulders
Cast off 6(6:7) sts at beg of next 4 rows, then 6(7:6) sts at beg of
foll 2 rows.
Cast off rem 22(24:26) sts.

LEFT FRONT

With 3¾mm (No 9/US 4) needles and M, cast on 67(69:71) sts.
Mst row (right side): K1, [p1, k1] to end.
Mst a further 5 rows. **
Next row: K to last 5 sts, k1, [p1, k1] twice.
Next row: K1, [p1, k1] twice, p to end.
Rep last 2 rows until work measures 14(16:18.5)cm/5(6½:7¼)in
from beg, ending with a right side row.
Dec row: K1, [p1, k1] twice, p4(5:6), * p2tog, p2tog, p1*; work
from * to * 3 times more, p2tog, p3tog, work from * to * 4 times,
p2tog, p2tog, p9(10:11). 46(48:50) sts.
Work cable and bobble panel thus:
1st row: K10(11:12), * p2, C4B, p5, k2, MB, k2, p5 , C4F, p2 *,
k5(6:7), [p1, k1] twice.
2nd row: K1, [p1, k1] twice, p4(5:6), * k2, p4, k5, p5, k5, p4, k2 *,
p10(11:12).
3rd row: K10(11:12), * p2, k4, p5, MB, k3, MB, p5, k4, p2 *,
k5(6:7), [p1, k1] twice.
4th row: As 2nd row.
5th and 6th rows: As 1st and 2nd rows.
7th row: K10(11:12), * p2, k4, p4, T3B, p1, T3F, p4, k4, p2 *,
k5(6:7), [p1, k1] twice.
8th row: K1, [p1, k1] twice, p4 (5:6), * k2, p4, k4, p2, k1, p1, k1,
p2, k4, p4, k2 *, p10(11:12).

9th row: K10(11:12), * p2, C4B, p3, T3B, k1, p1, k1, T3F, p3, C4F, p2 *, k5(6:7), [p1, k1] twice.

10th row: K1, [p1, k1] twice, p4(5:6), * k2, p4, k3, p3, k1, p1, k1, p3, k3, p4, k2 *, p10(11:12).

11th row: K10(11:12), * p2, k4, p2, T3B, p1, [k1, p1] twice, T3F, p2, k4, p2 *, k5(6:7), [p1, k1] twice.

12th row: K1, [p1, k1] twice, p4(5:6), * k2, p4, k2, p2, k1, [p1, k1] 3 times, p2, k2, p4, k2 *, p10(11:12).

13th row: K10(11:12), * p2, C4B, p2, k3, p1, [k1, p1] twice, k3, p2, C4F, p2 *, k5(6:7), [p1, k1] twice.

14th row: As 12th row.

15th row: K10(11:12),* p2, k4, p2, T3F, p1, [k1, p1] twice, T3B, p2, k4, p2 *, k5(6:7), [p1, k1] twice.

16th row: As 10th row.

17th row: K10(11:12), * p2, C4B, p3, T3F, k1, p1, k1, T3B, p3, C4F, p2 *, k5(6:7), [p1, k1] twice.

18th row: As 8th row.

19th row: K10(11:12), * p2, k4, p4, T3F, p1, T3B, p4, k4, p2 *, k5(6:7), [p1, k1] twice.

20th row: K1, [p1, k1] twice, p5(6:7), * k2, p4, k5, p5, k5, p4, k2 *, p10(11:12).

These 20 rows form the cable and bobble patt with mst front border.

Patt a further 16 rows.

Shape armhole

Next row: Cast off 3 sts, patt to end.

Patt 1 row.

Dec 1 st at armhole edge on the next 3 rows. 40(42:44) sts.

Patt a further 24 rows.

Dec row: K1, [p1, k1] twice, p5(6:7), p2tog, p2tog, p4, p2tog, p1, p2tog, p2, p2tog, p4, p2tog, p2tog, p5(6:7). 33(35:37) sts.

Keeping continuity of 5-st mst border, work 3(5:7) rows in st st.

*** Shape neck

Next row: K1, [p1, k1] twice, p3 and leave these 8 sts on a safety-pin, work to end. 25(27:29) sts.

Work 1 row.

Keeping continuity in st st, cast off 4(5:6) sts at beg of next row. 21(22:23) sts.

Dec 1 st at neck edge on the next 3 rows. 18(19:20) sts.

Work 5(7:9) rows in st st.

Shape shoulder

Cast off 6(6:7) sts at beg of next and foll alt row.

Work 1 row.

Cast off rem 6(7:6) sts.

RIGHT FRONT

Work as left front to **.

Next row: K1, [p1, k1] twice, k to end.

Next row: P to last 5 sts, k1, [p1, k1] twice.

Rep last 2 rows until work measures 12.5(12.5:14.5)cm/5(5:5¾)in from beg, ending with a wrong side row.

Buttonhole row: K1, p2tog, yrn, work to end.

Cont as before until work measures 14(16:18.5)cm/5½(6¼:7¼)in from beg, ending with a wrong side row.

Dec row: P9(10:11), p2tog, p2tog, * p1, p2tog, p2tog *; work from * to * 3 times more, p3tog, p2tog, work from * to * 4 times, p4(5:6), k1, [p1, k1] twice. 46 (48:50) sts.

Work cable and bobble patt thus:

1st row (right side): K1, [p1, k1] twice, k4(5:6), work from * to * on 1st row of left front, k10(11:12).

2nd row: P10(11:12), work from * to * on 2nd row of of left front, p4(5:6), k1, [p1, k1] twice.

3rd row: K1, [p1, k1] twice, k4(5:6), work from * to * on 3rd row of left front, k10(11:12).

4th row: P10(11:12), work from * to * on 4th row of left front, p4(5:6), k1, [p1, k1] twice.

These 4 rows set position of the cable and bobble patt.

Keeping continuity of patt as set to match left front, patt a further 33 rows, working a buttonhole as before on the 9th(1st:1st) of these rows and on the 1(2:2) foll 18th(16th:16th) row.

Shape armhole

Next row: Cast off 3 sts, patt to end.

Dec 1 st at armhole edge on next 3 rows. 40(42:44) sts.

Patt a further 24 rows, working a buttonhole on the 8th(12th:12th) of these rows.

Dec row: P5(6:7), p2tog, p2tog, p4, p2tog, p2, p2tog, p1, p2tog, p4, p2tog, p2tog, p5(6:7), k1, [p1, k1] twice. 33 (35:37) sts.

Keeping continuity of 5-st mst border, work 4(6:8) rows, working a buttonhole on the 1st(3rd:3rd) of these rows.

Work as left front from *** to end

SLEEVES

With 3¾mm (No 9/US 4) needles and M, cast on 53(65:69) sts.

Work 2 rows in mst as given for back, inc 1 st in centre of last row. 54 (66:70) sts.

Beg with a k row, work in st st for 3(5:5) rows.

Dec row: [P1, p3tog] 1(1:2) time(s), [p1, p2tog] 1(0:0) time, p2(4:2), * [p3tog, p1] twice, p2tog, p3; rep from * 2(3:3) times more, [p3tog, p1] 1(1:2) time(s), p2(2:0). 34(42:42) sts.

Work 9 rows in smock pattern as given for 1st size of back.

Inc row: P3, * m1, p4(7:4); rep from * to last 3(4:3) sts, m1, p to end. 42(48:52) sts.

Beg with a k row, work in st st for 0(4:0) rows.

Cont in st st, inc 1 st each end of next row and the 11(11:12) foll 4th rows. 66(72:78) sts.

Cont in st st until sleeve measures 24(26:28)cm/9½(10¼:11)in from beg, ending with a p row.

Cast off.

COLLAR

Join shoulder seams. With right side facing, using 3¼mm (No 10/US 3) needles, sl 8 sts from right front safety-pin on to needle, rejoin M and pick up and k20(22:22) sts up right front neck, 30(34:34) sts across back neck and 20(22:22) sts down left front neck, then patt across the 8 sts on left front safety-pin. 86(94:94) sts.

Next row: Cast off 3 sts, k next st, p5, [C2B, p6] to last 12 sts, C2B, p5, k1, [p1, k1] twice.

Next row: Cast off 3 sts, k next st, p1, k3, Cr2L, Cr2R, [k4, Cr2L, Cr2R] to last 6 sts, k3, p1, k1, p1. 80(88:88) sts.

Next row: P1, k1, p1, [p2, Cr2R, p2, Cr2L] to last 5 sts, p3, k1, p1.

Next row: P1, k1, p1, k1, [Cr2L, k4, Cr2R] to last 4 sts, k1, p1, k1, p1.

These 4 rows set position of the smock patt, with 3 edge sts worked in mst.

Patt a further 3 rows.

Change to 3¾mm (No 9/US 4) needles and work in patt for a further 10 rows.

Next row: Mst 3 sts, work 2tog, * mst 7(6:6) sts, work 2tog; rep from * to last 3 sts, mst to end. 71(77:77) sts.

Mst 3 rows.

Cast off loosely in mst.

TO MAKE UP

Set in sleeves, sewing the last 4 row ends to cast off sts at underarms. Join side and sleeve seams. Using contrasting shade, embroider smocking effect on smock patt areas on back, collar and sleeves, by working 3 back sts over each C2B and C2F and single k sts at side edges. Sew on buttons.

Herringbone and Moss Stitch Sweater

MATERIALS

21(22:23:24:25) 50g balls of Rowan Denim.
Pair each of 3¼mm (No 10/US 3) and 4mm (No 8/US 6) knitting needles.

MEASUREMENTS

To fit bust/chest sizes	81-86	91-97	102-107	112	117cm
	32-34	36-38	40-42	44	46in
Actual measurement	1·17	123	127	133	137cm
	46	48¼	50	52¼	54in
Length	67	69.5	69.5	69.5	69.5cm
	26¼	27¼	27¼	27¼	27¼in
Sleeve seam with	47	47	52	52	52cm
cuff turned back	18½	18½	20½	20½	20½in

TENSION BEFORE WASHING

See basic information on page 7.
20 sts and 28 rows to 10cm/4in square over st st on 4mm (No 8/US 6) needles.

NOTE

Read chart from right to left on right side rows and from left to right on wrong side rows.

ABBREVIATIONS

See page 7.

BACK

With 3¼mm (No 10/US 3) needles, cast on 117 (123:129:135:135) sts.
1st rib row: K3, [p3, k3] to end.
2nd rib row: P3, [k3, p3] to end.
Rep last 2 rows, 12 times more, dec 1 st each end of the last row on the 3rd and 4th sizes only and inc 1 st each end of the 5th size only. 117(123:127:133:137) sts.
Change to 4mm (No 8/US 6) needles.
Beg with a k row, work in st st for 49(52:52:52:52)cm/19¼(20½:20½:20½:20½)in from beg, ending with a p row, dec 6 sts evenly across last row. 111(117: 121:127:131) sts.
Beg with the 1st row, reading odd-numbered rows from right to left and even-numbered rows from left to right, work from chart until work measures 57(60:60:60:60)cm/22½(23½:23½:23½:23½)in from beg, ending with a wrong side row.
Shape armholes
1st and 2nd rows: Cast off 4 sts, work to end.
3rd row: K4, k3tog, work to last 7 sts, k3tog tbl, k4.
4th row: Work to end.

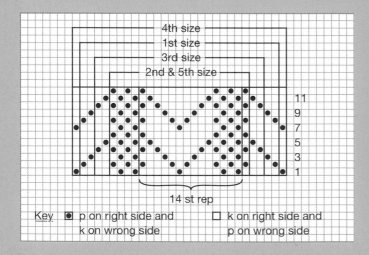

4th size
1st size
3rd size
2nd & 5th size

11
9
7
5
3
1

14 st rep

Key ■ p on right side and k on wrong side   □ k on right side and p on wrong side

5th to 9th rows: Rep 3rd and 4th rows, twice more, then work 3rd row again. 87(93:97:103:107) sts.
Cont in patt until work measures 83(87:87:87:87)cm/32¾(34¼:34¼:34¼:34¼)in from beg, ending with a wrong side row.

Divide for neck
Next row: Patt 31(34:36:37:39) sts, turn and leaving rem sts on a spare needle, work on these sts for right back neck.

Right back neck
Next row: Cast off 4 sts, patt to end.
Leave rem 27(30:32:33:35) sts on a spare needle.

Left back neck
With right side facing, cast off centre 25(25:25:29:29) sts, rejoin yarn to inner edge of rem sts and patt to end.
Patt 1 row,
Next row: Cast off 4 sts, patt to end.
Leave rem 27(30:32:33:35) sts on a spare needle.

FRONT
Work as back until work measures 73(77:77:77:77)cm/28¾(30¼:30¼:30¼:30¼)in from beg, ending with a wrong side row.

Divide for neck
Patt 38(41:43:46:48) sts, turn and leaving rem sts on a spare needle, work on these sts for left front neck.

Left front neck
Next row: Cast off 5 sts, patt to end.
Dec 1 st at neck edge on next row and the 5(5:5:7:7) foll alt rows. 27 (30:32:33:35) sts.
Cont in patt until work measures the same as back to shoulder, ending with a wrong side row.
Leave rem sts on a spare needle.

Right front neck
With right side facing, sl centre 11 sts on to a st-holder, rejoin yarn to inner edge of sts on spare needle and patt to end.
Work as given for left front neck.

SLEEVES
With 3¼mm (No 10/US 3) needles, cast on 57(57:63:63:63) sts.
Work 50 rows in rib as given for back.
Change to 4mm (No 8/US 6) needles.
Beg with a k row, st st 4(4:6:6:6) rows.
Cont in st st, inc 1 st each end of next row and the 4(4:5:5:5) foll 5th(5th:7th:7th:7th) rows. 67(67:75:75:75) sts.
Patt 3(3:5:5:5) rows.
Inc 1 st each end of next row and the 16(16:12:12:12) foll 6th(6th:8th:8th:8th) rows. 101 sts.
Cont in st st until work measures 68.5(68.5:74.5:74.5:74.5)cm/27(27:29¼:29¼:29¼)in from beg, ending with a wrong side row.

Shape sleeve top
Work as given for armhole shaping on back when 77 sts will remain.
Work 1 row.
Cast off.

COLLAR
Join right shoulder seam, by casting off sts tog on right side to form a ridge. With right side facing, using 3¼mm (No 10/US 3) needles, pick up and k23(25:25:27:27) sts down left front neck, k11 sts at centre front inc 0(2:2:1:1) sts evenly, pick up and k23(25:25:27:27) sts up right front neck and k30(30:30:39:39) sts from centre back neck. 87(93:93:105:105) sts.
Beg with the 2nd row, work 24 rows in rib as given for back.
Change to 4mm (No 8/US 6) needles and work a further 36 rows in rib.
Cast off in rib.

TO MAKE UP
First, see basic information on page 7. Then join left shoulder seam, by casting off sts tog on right side to form a ridge. Join collar, reversing seam to allow for fold back. Set sleeves into armholes. Join side and sleeve seams reversing seam on cuff.

Lace Jacket

MATERIALS
7(8:9) 50g balls of Rowan True 4 ply Botany.
Pair of 3¾mm (No 9/US 4) knitting needles.
7 buttons.

MEASUREMENTS

To fit bust sizes	81-86	91-97	102-107cm
	32-34	36-38	40-42in
Actual measurement	93	105	118cm
	36½	41¾	46½in
Length	57	58	60cm
	22½	23	23½in
Sleeve seam	41.5	41.5	41.5cm
	16¼	16¼	16¼in

TENSION
25 sts and 36 rows to 10cm/4in square over patt on 3¾mm (No 9/US 4) needles.

ABBREVIATIONS
See page 7.

BACK
With 3¾mm (No 9/US 4) needles, cast on 113(129:145) sts.
P 4 rows.
1st row (right side): K1, [yf, skpo, k11, k2tog, yf, k1] to end.
2nd and every foll alt row: P to end.
3rd row: K2, [yf, skpo, k9, k2tog, yf, k3] to last 15 sts, yf, skpo, k9, k2tog, yf, k2.
5th row: K3, [yf, skpo, k7, k2tog, yf, k5] to last 14 sts, yf, skpo, k7, k2tog, yf, k3.
7th row: K4, [yf, skpo, k5, k2tog, yf, k7] to last 13 sts, yf, skpo, k5, k2tog, yf, k4.
9th row: K5, [yf, skpo, k3, k2tog, yf, k9] to last 12 sts, yf, skpo, k3, k2tog, yf, k5.
11th row: K6, [yf, skpo, k1, k2tog, yf, k11] to last 11 sts, yf, skpo, k1, k2tog, yf, k6.
13th row: K7, [yf, sl 1, k2tog, psso, yf, k13] to last 10 sts, yf, sl 1, k2tog, psso, yf, k7.
14th row: P to end.
These 14 rows form the patt for the back.
Patt a further 2 rows.
1st dec row: Patt 7, [skpo, patt 14] to last 10 sts, skpo, patt 8. 106(121:136) sts.
Keeping continuity of patt, patt 3 rows.
2nd dec row: Patt 7, [k2tog, patt 13] to last 9 sts, k2tog, patt 7. 99(113:127) sts.
Patt 5 rows.
Next row: K1, [yf, skpo, k9, k2tog, yf, k1] to end.
Patt a further 13 rows as set.

3rd dec row: Patt 6, [skpo, patt 12] to last 9 sts, skpo, patt 7. 92(105:118) sts.
Patt 3 rows.
4th dec row: Patt 6, [k2tog, patt 11] to last 8 sts, k2tog, patt 6. 85(97:109) sts.
Patt 3 rows.
Next row: K1, [yf, skpo, k7, k2tog, yf, k1] to end.
Patt a further 21 rows as set.
1st inc row: Patt 6, [inc, patt 11] to last 7 sts, inc, patt 6. 92(105:118) sts.
Patt 3 rows.
2nd inc row: Patt 6, [inc, patt 12] to last 8 sts, inc, patt 7. 99(113:127) sts.
Patt 5 rows.
Next row: K1, [yf, skpo, k9, k2tog, yf, k1] to end.
Patt 25 rows as set.
3nd inc row: Patt 7, [inc, patt 13] to last 8 sts, inc, patt 7. 106(121:136) sts.
Patt 3 rows.
4th inc row: Patt 7, [inc, patt 14] to last 9 sts, inc, patt 8. 113(129:145) sts.
Patt 7 rows.
Next row: K1, [yf, skpo, k11, k2tog, yf, k1] to end.
Patt 23 rows as set.

Shape armholes
Keeping continuity of patt as set, cast off 7 sts at beg of next 2 rows.
Dec 1 st each end of next 5 rows, then on the 4 foll alt rows. 81(97:113) sts.
Patt a further 47(51:55) rows.

Shape shoulders
Cast off 11(14:17) at beg of next 4 rows.
Cast off rem 37(41:45) sts.

LEFT FRONT
With 3¾mm (No 9 (US/ 4) needles, cast on 62 (70:78) sts.
P 4 rows. **
1st row (right side): K1, [yf, skpo, k11, k2tog, yf, k1] to last 13(5:13) sts, [yf, skpo, k6] 1(0:1) time, p5.
2nd and every alternate row: P to end.
3rd row: K2, [yf, skpo, k9, k2tog, yf, k3] to last 12(20:12) sts, yf, skpo, k5(9:5), [k2tog, yf, k2] 0(1:0) time, p5.
5th row: K3, [yf, skpo, k7, k2tog, yf, k5] to last 11(19:11) sts, yf, skpo, k4(7:4), [k2tog, yf, k3] 0(1:0) time, p5.
7th row: K4, [yf, skpo, k5, k2tog, yf, k7] to last 10(18:10) sts, yf, skpo, k3(5:3), [k2tog, yf, k4] 0(1:0) time, p5.
9th row: K5, [yf, skpo, k3, k2tog, yf, k9] to last 9(17:9) sts, yf, skpo, k2(3:2), [k2tog, yf, k5] 0(1:0) time, p5.
11th row: K6, [yf, skpo, k1, k2tog, yf, k11] to last 8(16:8) sts, yf, skpo, k1, [k2tog, yf, k6] 0(1:0) time, p5.
13th row: K7, [yf, sl 1, k2tog, psso, yf, k13] to last 7(15:7) sts, [yf, skpo] 1(0:1) time, [yf, sl 1, k2tog, psso, yf, k7] 0(1:0) time, p5.
14th row: P to end.

These 14 rows form the patt for the left front.

Patt a further 2 rows.

1st dec row: Patt 7, [skpo, patt 14] to last 7(15:7) sts, skpo, patt 5(13:5). 58(66:73) sts.

Patt 3 rows.

2nd dec row: Patt 7, [k2tog, patt 13] to last 21(14:21) sts, k2tog, patt 19(12:19). 55(62:69) sts.

Patt 19 rows.

3rd dec row: Patt 6, [skpo, patt 12] to last 7(14:7) sts, skpo, patt 5(12:5). 51(58) (64) sts.

Patt 3 rows.

4th dec row: Patt 6, [k2tog, patt 11] to last 19(13:19) sts, k2tog, patt 17(11:17). 48(54:60) sts.

Patt 25 rows.

Ist inc row: Patt 6, [inc, patt 11] to last 18(12:18) sts, inc, patt 17(11:17). 51(58:64) sts.

Patt 3 rows.

2nd inc row: Patt 6, [inc, patt 12] to last 6(13:6) sts, inc, patt 5(12:5). 55 (62:69) sts.

Patt 31 rows.

3rd inc row: Patt 7, [inc, patt 13] to last 20 (13:20) sts, inc, patt 19(12:19). 58(66:73) sts.

Patt 3 rows.

4th inc row: Patt 7, [inc, patt 14] to last 6(14:6) sts, inc, patt 5(13:5). 62(70:78) sts.

Patt 31 rows.

Shape armhole and neck

Next row: Cast off 7 sts, patt to last 6 sts, p2tog, p4.

Next row: Patt to end.

*** Dec 1 st at armhole edge on each of the next 5 rows, then on the 4 foll alt rows, **at the same time**, dec 1 st at front edge inside a border of 4 sts on the 1st of these rows and the 6 foll alt rows. 38(46:54) sts.

Patt 2 rows. ***

Next row: P4, p2tog, patt to end.

Patt 2 rows.

Next row: Patt to last 6 sts, p2tog, p4.

**** Patt 2 rows.

Cont to dec at front edge as before on next row and the 8(10:12) foll 3rd rows. 27(33:39) sts.

Patt 14(12:10) rows.

Patt 15(13:11) rows here for right front.

Shape shoulder

Cast off 11(14:17) sts at beg of next row and foll alt row. 5 sts.

P1 row, inc 1 st at inside edge. 6 sts.

Cont in gst (every row p) until band fits across to centre back neck. Cast off.

RIGHT FRONT

Work as left front to **.

1st row (right side): P5, [k6, k2tog, yf] 1(0:1) time, k1, [yf, skpo, k11, k2tog, yf, k1] to end.

2nd and every alternate row: P to end.

3rd row: P5, [k2, yf, skpo] 0(1:0) time, k5(9:5), k2tog, yf, [k3, yf, skpo, k9, k2tog, yf] to last 2 sts, k2.

5th row: P5, [k3, yf, skpo] 0(1:0) time, k4(7:4), k2tog, yf, [k5, yf, skpo, k7, k2tog, yf] to last 3 sts, k3.

7th row: P5, [k4, yf, skpo] 0(1:0) time, k3(5:3), k2tog, yf, [k7, yf, skpo, k5, k2tog, yf] to last 4 sts, k4.

9th row: P5, [k5, yf, skpo] 0(1:0) time, k2(3:2), k2tog, yf, [k9, yf, skpo, k3, k2tog, yf] to last 5 sts, k5.

11th row: P5, [k6, yf, skpo] 0(1:0) time, k1, k2tog, yf, [k11, yf, skpo, k1, k2tog, yf] to last 6 sts, k6.

13th row: P5, [k7, yf, sl 1, k2tog, psso, yf] 0(1:0) time, [k2tog, yf] 1(0:1) time, [k13, yf, sl 1, k2tog, psso, yf] to last 7 sts, k7.

14th row: P to end.

These 14 rows form the patt for the right front.

Patt a further 2 rows.

1st dec and buttonhole row: P1, p2tog, yrn, p2 for buttonhole, then patt 15(7:15), [skpo, patt 14] to last 10 sts, skpo, k8. 59(66:74) sts.

Patt 3 rows.

2nd dec row: Patt 5(12:5), [k2tog, patt 13] to last 9 sts, k2tog, patt 7. 55(62:69) sts.

Patt 19 rows, working a buttonhole as before on the 16th of these rows.

3rd dec row: Patt 18(11:18), [skpo, patt 12] to last 9 sts, skpo, patt 7. 52(58:65) sts.

Patt 3 rows.

4th dec row: Patt 5(11:5), [k2tog, patt 11] to last 8 sts, k2tog, patt 6. 48(54:60) sts.

Patt 25 rows, making a buttonhole on the 12th of these rows.

Inc row: Patt 5(11:5), [inc, patt 11] to last 7 sts, inc, patt 6. 52(58:65) sts.

Patt 3 rows.

2nd inc row: Patt 18(11:18), [inc, patt 12] to last 8 sts, inc, patt 7. 55(62:69) sts.

Patt 31 rows, making a buttonhole on the 2nd and 22nd of these rows.

3rd inc row: Patt 5(12:5), [inc, patt 13] to last 8 sts, inc, patt 7. 59(66:74) sts.

Patt 3 rows.

4th inc row: Patt 20(12:20), [inc, patt 14] to last 9 sts, inc, patt 8. 62(70:78) sts.

Patt 31 rows, making a buttonhole on the 6th and 26th of these rows.

Shape armhole and neck

Next row: P4, p2tog tbl, patt to end.

Next row: Cast off 7 sts, patt to end.

Work as left front from *** to ***.

Next row: P to last 6 sts, p2tog tbl, p4.

Patt 2 rows.

Next row: P4, p2tog tbl, patt to end.

Work as left front from **** to end, noting variation.

SLEEVES

With 3¾mm (No 9 /US 4) needles, cast on 49(53:53) sts.

P 4 rows.

1st row (right side): K1(8:8), [k2tog, yf, k1] 0(1:1) time, [yf, skpo, k11, k2tog, yf, k1] to last 0(10:10) sts, [yf, skpo] 0(1:1) time, k0(8:8).

2nd row: P to end.

3rd row: K2(7:7), [k2tog, yf, k3] 0 (1:1) time, [yf, skpo, k9, k2tog, yf, k3] to last 15(9:9) sts, yf, skpo, k9(7:7), [k2tog, yf, k2] 1(0:0) time.

4th row: P to end.

These 4 rows set the patt for the sleeves. Keeping continuity of patt, taking extra sts into patt as they occur, inc 1 st each end of the next row and the 15(21:21) foll 8th(6th:6th) rows. 81(97:97) sts.

Patt 21(15:15) rows.

Shape top

Cast off 7 sts at beg of next 2 rows.

Dec 1 st each end of next row and the 2(0:2) foll 4th rows.

Patt 1 row, then dec 1 st each end of next row and the 4(11:9) foll alt rows. 51(57:57) sts.

Patt 1 row, then dec 1 st each end of the next 7 rows.

Patt 1 row.

Cast off 3(4:4) sts at beg of next 6 rows.

Cast off rem 19 sts.

TO MAKE UP

Join shoulder seams. Set in sleeves. Join side and sleeve seams. Sew band to back neck, and join seam. Sew on buttons.

Lace Alpaca Scarf

MATERIALS
3 x 50g balls of Jaeger Alpaca 4 ply.
Pair of 4mm (No 8/US 6) knitting needles.

MEASUREMENT
Approximately 26 x 120cm/10¼ x 47¼in.

TENSION
29 sts and 32 rows to 10cm/4in square over patt on 4mm
(No 8/US 6) needles.

ABBREVIATIONS
See page 7.

TO MAKE
With 4mm (No 8/US 6) needles, cast on 77 sts.
K1 row, then work patt.
1st row (right side): K7, * yf, k2tog, k6; rep from * to last 6 sts, yf,
k2tog, k4.
2nd row: K2, p to last 2 sts, k2.
3rd row: K5, * k2tog tbl, yf, k1, yf, k2tog, k3; rep from * to end.
4th row: K2, p to last 2 sts, k2.
5th row: K4, * k 2tog tbl, yf, k3, yf, k2tog, k1; rep from * to last st,
k1.
6th row: As 4th row.
7th row: K2, * yf, k2tog tbl, then place st just worked back on to
left-hand needle, pass next st on left-hand needle over this st, now
place st back on to right-hand needle, yf, k5; rep from * to last 3
sts, k3.
8th row: As 4th row.
9th row: K3, * inc, k7; rep from * to last 2 sts, k2.
10th row: As 4th row.
11th row: K2, * k2tog, k4, yf, k2tog, k1; rep from * to last 3 sts, k3.
12th row: K2, p to last 2 sts, k2.
The 3rd to 12th rows form the patt.
Cont in patt until scarf measures 120cm/47¼in, ending with the
11th row.
K1 row.
Cast off.

Child's Zipped Jacket

MATERIALS

6(8) 50g hanks of Rowan DK Tweed in Oatmeal (M).
1 50g hank of the same yarn in each of Dark Blue, Light Blue, Pale Green, Red and Light Pink.
Pair each of 3¼mm (No 10/US 3) and 4mm (No 8/US 6) knitting needles.
An open-ended zip fastener of appropriate length.

MEASUREMENTS

To fit ages	3-4	4-5 years
Actual chest measurement	81	90cm
	32	35½in
Length	40	44cm
	15¾	17¼in
Sleeve seam	22.5	27.5cm
	8¾	10¾in

TENSION

22 sts and 30 rows to 10cm/4in square over st st on 4mm (No 8/US 6) needles.

ABBREVIATIONS

See page 7.

NOTES

Read chart from right to left on right side (K) rows and from left to right on wrong side (P) rows. When working pattern, strand yarn not in use loosely across back of work to keep fabric elastic.

BACK

With 3¼mm (No 10/US 3) needles and M, cast on 91(101) sts.
Mst row: K1, [p1, k1] to end.
Rep last row, 5 times more.
Change to 4mm (No 8/US 6) needles.
Beg with a k row, st st 70(78) rows.
Beg with the 1st row, work in patt from chart until all 17 rows have been completed.
Mark each end of the 2nd of these rows to denote end of side seams.
Cont in M only and st st a further 27(31) rows.

Shape shoulders

Cast off 16(18) sts at beg of next 4 rows.
Cast off rem 27(29) sts.

POCKET LININGS (Make 2)

With 4mm (No 8/US 6) needles and M, cast on 21 sts.
Beg with a k row, st st 30 rows.
Leave sts on a st holder.

LEFT FRONT

With 3¼mm (No 10/US 3) needles and M, cast on 45(49) sts.
Work 6 rows in mst as given for back.
Change to 4mm (No 8/US 6) needles. **
1st row (right side): K to last 4 sts, for front edging, mst 4.
2nd row: For front edging, mst 4, p to end.
Rep last 2 rows, 11 times more, then work the 1st row again.
Next row: Mst 4, p10(12), [k1, p1] 10 times, k1, p10(12).
Next row: K11(13), [p1, k1] 10 times, k10(12), mst 4.
Rep last 2 rows, once more.
1st pocket row: Mst 4, p10(12), cast off 21 sts in mst, p to end.
2nd pocket row: K10(12), k the 21 sts of one pocket lining, k to last 4 sts, mst 4. 45(49) sts.

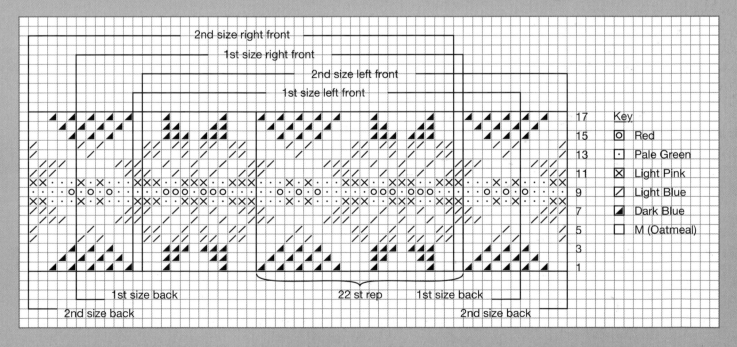

Key
O	Red
·	Pale Green
X	Light Pink
/	Light Blue
◢	Dark Blue
☐	M (Oatmeal)

Keeping the 4 sts at front edge in mst, work a further 39(47) rows.
*** Beg with the 1st row and keeping 4 sts at front edge in M and mst, work in patt from chart until all 17 rows have been completed. Mark side edge of the 2nd of these rows to denote end of side seam.

Keeping the 4 sts at front edge in mst, cont with M only and work a further 11(15) rows.***

Shape neck

Next row: Work to last 6 sts, work 2tog, turn and leave the 4 edge sts on a safety-pin.

Work 1 row.

Dec 1 st at neck edge on next row and the 6 foll alt rows. 33(37) sts.

Work 1 row.

Shape shoulder and cont to shape neck

Next row: Cast off 16(18) sts, k to last 2 sts, dec. 16(18) sts.

Work 1 row.

Cast off rem 16(18) sts.

RIGHT FRONT

Work as left front to **.

1st row (right side): For front edging, mst 4, k to end.

2nd row: P to last 4 sts, for front edging, mst 4.

Rep last 2 rows, 11 times more, then work the 1st row again.

Next row: P10(12), k1, [p1, k1] 10 times, p10(12), mst 4.

Next row: Mst 4, k11(13), [p1, k1] 10 times, k10(12).

Rep last 2 rows, once more.

1st pocket row: P10(12), cast off 21 sts in mst, p10(12), mst 4.

2nd pocket row: Mst 4, k 10 (12), k the 21 sts of other pocket lining, k to end.

Keeping the 4 sts at front edge in mst, work a further 39(47) rows. Work as left front from *** to ***.

Shape neck

Next row: Mst 4 and leave on a safety-pin, work 2tog, work to end.

Work 1 row.

Dec 1 st at neck edge on next row and the 7 foll alt rows. 32(36) sts.

Shape shoulder

Cast off 16(18) sts at beg of next row. 16(18) sts.

Work 1 row.

Cast off rem 16(18) sts.

SLEEVES

With 3¼mm (No 10/US 3) needles and M, cast on 33(37) sts.

Work 6 rows in mst as given for back.

Change to 4mm (No 8/US 6) needles.

Beg with a k row, st st 2 rows.

Cont in st st, inc 1 st each end of next row and the 13(15) foll 4th rows. 61(69) sts.

St st a further 7(13) rows.

Cast off.

RIGHT HALF COLLAR

First join shoulder seams.

With right side of work facing, using 3¼mm (No 10/US 3) needles and M, sl 4 sts from right front safety-pin onto needle, turn.

Mst 1 row.

**** Cont in mst and inc 1 st at inner edge on each of the next 7 rows. 11 sts.

Mst 1 row, then inc 1 st at inner edge on the next row and the 9 foll alt rows. 21 sts.

Cont in mst until collar fits up front neck to shoulder, ending at outer edge.

Shape collar

Next 2 rows: Mst 12, turn, sl 1, mst to end.

Mst 6 rows straight.

Rep last 8 rows until collar fits when slightly stretched, across to centre back neck.

Cast off.

LEFT HALF COLLAR

With wrong side of work facing, using 3¼mm (No 10/US 3) needles and M, sl 4 sts from left front safety-pin onto needle, turn.

Rejoin yarn to inner edge and mst to end.

Mst 1 row.

Work as right half collar from **** to end.

TO MAKE UP

Sew cast-off edge of sleeves to row ends above markers on back and fronts. Join side and sleeve seams. Sew shaped edge of collar to neck edge, then join cast-off edges tog. Sew pocket linings to wrong side. Sew in zip fastener.

Cabled Hearts Sweater

MATERIALS

10(13) 50g balls of Rowan Denim.
Pair each of 3¼mm (No 10/US 3) and 4mm (No 8/US 6) knitting needles.
A set of four 3¼ mm (No 10/US 3) double pointed knitting needles.
A cable needle.

MEASUREMENTS

To fit ages	3-4	4-5 years
Actual measurement	88.5	96.5cm
	35¼	37¾in
Length	43.5	47.5cm
	17	18¾in
Sleeve seam	27.5	31cm
	10¾	12¼in

TENSION BEFORE WASHING

See basic information on page 7.
20 sts and 28 rows to 10cm/4in square over patt on 4mm (No 8/US 5) needles.

ABBREVIATIONS

C3B = Sl next st on to cable needle and leave at back of work, k2, then k st from cable needle.
C3F = Sl next 2 sts on to cable needle and leave at front of work, k1, then k2 from cable needle.
C4F = Sl next 2 sts on to cable needle and leave at front of work, k2, then k2 from cable needle.
Cr3R = Sl next st on to cable needle and leave at back of work, k2, then p st from cable needle.
Cr3L = Sl next 2 sts on to cable needle and leave at front of work, p1, then k2 from cable needle.
Cr4R = Sl next 2 sts on to cable needle and leave at back of work, k2, then p2 from cable needle.
Cr4L = Sl next 2 sts on to cable needle and leave at front of work, p2, then k2 from cable needle.
MB = K1, p1, k1, p1 all into same st, turn, sl 2, k2tog, then pass sl sts over, turn and sl st back on to right-hand needle.
Also see page 7.

1st size only
PANEL A (worked over 10 sts)
1st row (right side): P1, k1, p1, k4, p1, k1, p1.
2nd row: P1, k1, p6, k1, p1.
3rd row: P1, k1, p1, k4, p1, k1, p1.
4th row: P1, k1, p6, k1, p1.
5th row: P1, k1, p1, C4F, p1, k1, p1.
6th row: P1, k1, p6, k1, p1.
These 6 rows form the patt for panel A.

2nd size only
PANEL A (worked over 12 sts)
1st row (right side): [K1, p1] twice, k4, [p1, k1] twice.
2nd row: K1, p1, k1, p6, k1, p1, k1.
3rd row: [K1, p1] twice, k4, [p1, k1] twice.
4th row: K1, p1, k1, p6, k1, p1, k1.
5th row: [K1, p1] twice, C4F, [p1, k1] twice.
6th row: K1, p1, k1, p6, k1, p1, k1.
These 6 rows form the patt for panel A.

PANEL B (worked over 21 sts)
1st row (right side): P7, Cr3R, k1, Cr3L, p7.
2nd row: K7, p3, k1, p3, k7.
3rd row: P6, C3B, p1, k1, p1, C3F, p6.
4th row: K6, p2, k1, [p1, k1] twice, p2, k6.
5th row: P5, Cr3R, k1, [p1, k1] twice, Cr3L, p5.
6th row: K5, p3, k1, [p1, k1] twice, p3, k5.
7th row: P4, C3B, p1, [k1, p1] 3 times, C3F, p4.
8th row: K4, p2, k1, [p1, k1] 4 times, p2, k4.
9th row: P3, Cr3R, k1, [p1, k1] 4 times, Cr3L, p3.
10th row: K3, p3, k1, [p1, k1] 4 times, p3, k3.
11th row: P2, C3B, p1, [k1, p1] 5 times, C3F, p2.
12th row: K2, p2, k1, [p1, k1] 6 times, p2, k2.
13th row: P1, Cr3R, k1, [p1, k1] 6 times, Cr3L, p1.
14th row: K1, p3, k1, [p1, k1] 6 times, p3, k1.
15th row: P1, k2, p1, [k1, p1] 7 times, k2, p1.
16th row: K1, p3, k1, [p1, k1] 6 times, p3, k1.
17th row: P1, Cr4L, p1, [k1, p1] 5 times, Cr4R, p1.
18th row: K3, p3, k1, [p1, k1] 4 times, p3, k3.
19th row: P3, Cr4L, p1, k1, p1, MB, p1, k1, p1, Cr4R, p3.
20th row: K8, p2, k1, p2, k8.
These 20 rows form the patt for panel B.

BACK

With 4mm (No 8/US 6) needles, cast on 103(111) sts.
1st row (right side): Work 1st row of panel A, [work 1st row of panel B, then work 1st row of panel A] 3 times.
This row sets position of the panels.
Cont in patt until 138(150) rows have been completed.
Shape shoulders
Cast off 36(38) sts at beg of next 2 rows.
Leave rem 31(35) sts on a spare needle.

FRONT

Work as given for back until 122(134) rows have been completed.
Shape neck
Next row: Patt 41(43) sts, turn and leaving rem sts on a st holder, work on these sts for left front neck.
Left front neck: Patt 1 row.
Dec 1 st at neck edge on next row and the 4 foll alt rows. 36(38) sts.
Patt 5 rows straight.
Cast off for shoulder.
Right front neck: With right side of work facing, sl centre 21(25)

sts on to a st holder, rejoin yarn to inner edge of rem 41(43) sts and patt to end of row.
Patt 1 row.
Dec 1 st at neck edge on next row and the 4 foll alt rows. 36(38) sts.
Patt a further 6 rows.
Cast off for shoulder.

SLEEVES

With 3¼mm (No 10/US 3) needles, cast on 40 sts.
1st mst row (right side): [K1, p1] to end.
2nd mst row: [P1, k1] to end.
Rep last 2 rows, twice more, then work the 1st row again.
Inc row: P1, m1, p2, m1, [mst 7, m1, p2, m1] to last st, k1.
50 sts.
Change to 4 mm (No 8/US 6) needles.
1st row: Mst 1, [k4, mst 7] to last 5 sts, k4, mst 1.
2nd row: Mst 1, [p4, mst 7] to last 5 sts, p4, mst 1.
3rd row: Mst 1, [C4F, mst 7] to last 5 sts, C4F, mst 1.
4th row: As 2nd row.
5th row: As 1st row.
6th row: As 2nd row.
These 6 rows form the patt for the sleeves.
Keeping continuity of patt, taking extra sts into patt as they occur, inc 1 st at each end of the next row and the 12(14) foll 6th rows. 76(80) sts.
Patt a further 11(9) rows.
Cast off.

COLLAR

First join shoulder seams.
With right side facing, using set of four 3¼mm (No 10/US 3) double pointed needles, sl first 10(12) sts from centre front st holder on to a safety-pin, rejoin yarn to rem sts and k2tog, k9(11), pick up and k19 sts up right front neck, k the 31(35) sts at back neck, increasing 2 sts evenly, pick up and k19 sts down left front neck, then k the 10(12) sts from safety-pin. 91(99) sts.
Arrange the sts evenly on 3 needles.
Working backwards and forwards in rows, and using 4th needle, cont thus:
Mst row: K1, [p1, k1] to end.
Rep last row for 7(9)cm/2¾(3½)in.
Cast off in mst.

LOWER EDGING (make 2 pieces alike)

With 4mm (No 8/US 6) needles, cast on 99(110) sts.
1st mst row (right side): K1, [p1, k1] to last 0(1) st, p0(1).
2nd mst row: P0(1), [k1, p1] to last st, k1.
Next row: Mst 11, turn and work on these 11 sts thus:
*** Mst 1 row.
Dec 1 st each end of next and foll alt row. 7 sts.
Mst 1 row.
Next row: Dec, mst 1, MB, mst 1, dec. 5 sts.
Next row: Dec, mst 1, dec. 3 sts.

Next row: Mst 3 sts.
Next row: Sl 1, work 2tog, psso and fasten off. ***
With right side facing, rejoin yarn and patt 11, turn and work from *** to ***.
Work 7(8) more points in the same way.

TO MAKE UP

First, see basic information on page 7. Then mark side edges on back and from 19(20)cm/7½(8)in down from shoulder. Sew cast-off edge of sleeves to row-ends between markers on back and front. Join side and sleeve seams. Sew cast-on edge of edging to lower edge.

Cashmere Crossover Top

MATERIALS
13(14:15) 25g balls of Jaeger Cashmere 4 ply.
Pair each of 2¾mm (No 12/US 2) and 3¼mm (No 10/US 3) knitting needles.

MEASUREMENTS

To fit bust sizes	81	86	91cm
	32	34	36in
Actual measurement	87	92	97cm
	34¼	36¼	38in
Length	43	45	47cm
	17	17¾	18½in
Sleeve seam	44	44	44cm
	17¼	17¼	17¼in

TENSION
28 sts and 36 rows to 10cm/4in square over st st on 3¼mm (No 10/US 3) needles.

ABBREVIATIONS
See page 7.

BACK
With 2¾mm (No 12/US 2) needles, cast on 94(101:108) sts.
K9 rows.
Change to 3¼mm (No 10/US 3) needles and beg with a k row, work 4 rows in st st.
Inc row: K3, m1, k to last 3 sts, m1, k3. 96(103:110) sts.
Work 5 rows in st st.
Rep last 6 rows, 13 times more, then work the inc row again. 124(131:138) sts.
Cont in st st for another 1(3:7) row(s), work measures 26.5(27:28)cm/10¼(10½:11)in from beg, ending with a p row.
Shape armholes
Cast off 5 sts at beg of next 2 rows and 4 sts at beg of foll 2 rows.
Next row: K3, sl 1, k1, psso, k to last 5 sts, k2tog, k3.
Next row: P to end.
Rep last 2 rows, 9(10:11) times. 86(91:96) sts.
Cont in st st until work measures 43(45:47)cm/17(17¾:18½)in from beg, ending with a p row.
Shape shoulders
Cast off 11(12:13) sts at beg of next 4 rows.
Cast off rem 42(43:44) sts.

LEFT FRONT
With 2¾mm (No 12/US 2) needles, cast on 94(101:108) sts.
K9 rows.
Change to 3¼mm (No 10/US 3) needles.
1st row: K to end. **
2nd row: K4, p to end.

Rep last 2 rows, once.
Inc row: K3, m1, k to last 4 sts, m1, k4. 96(103:110) sts.
Work 5 rows as set.
Rep last 6 rows, 7 times more, then work the inc row again. 112(119:126) sts.
Shape front
1st and 2nd turning rows: K1, sl 1, turn, for 1st row, sl 1, k1 for 2nd row.
3rd and 4th turning rows: K2, sl 1, turn, for 3rd row, sl 1, k2 for 4th row.
5th and 6th turning rows: K3, sl 1, turn, for 5th row, sl 1, k3 for 6th row.
7th and 8th turning rows: K2, sl 1, turn, for 7th row, sl 1, k2 for 8th row.
9th and 10th turning rows: K1, sl 1, turn, for 9th row, sl 1, k1 for 10th row, turn.
Next row: K4 sts and leave on a safety-pin, p to end.
1st dec row: K to last 3 sts, k2tog, k1.
2nd dec row: P1, p2tog, p to end.
3rd dec row: K to last 3 sts, k2tog, k1.
4th dec row: P1, p2tog, p to end.
5th row: K3, m1, k to last 3 sts, k2tog, k1.
6th row: P1, p2tog, p to end.
Rep last 6 rows, 4 times more, then work the 1st to 5th rows again. 79*86:93) sts.
Work 1(3:7) rows, dec at neck edge on every row as before. Work measures 26.5(27:28)cm/10¼(10½:11)in from beg.
Shape armhole and cont to shape neck.
Next row: Cast off 5 sts, work to last 3 sts, work 2tog, k1.
Next row: P1, p2tog, work to end.
Next row: Cast off 4 sts, work to last 3 sts, work 2tog, k1.
Next row: P1 p2tog, work to end.
Next row: K3, sl 1, k1, psso, k to last 3 sts, k2tog, k1.
Next row: P1, p2tog, p to end.
*** Rep last 2 rows, 9(10:11) times more. 35(37:37) sts.
Keeping armhole edge straight, cont to dec at neck edge on every row until 22(24:26) sts rem. Cont without further shaping until work measures the same as back to shoulder, ending at side edge.
Shape shoulder
Cast off 11(12:13) sts at beg of next row.
Work 1 row.
Cast off rem 11(12:13) sts.

RIGHT FRONT
Work as left front to **.
Next row: P to last 4 sts, k4.
Rep last 2 rows, once more.
Inc row: K4, m1, k to last 3 sts, m1, k3. 96(103:110) sts.
Work 5 rows as set.
Rep last 6 rows, 7 times more. 112(119:126) sts.
Shape front
1st and 2nd turning rows: K1, sl 1, turn, for 1 st row, sl 1, k1 for 2nd row.

3rd and 4th turning rows: K2, sl 1, turn, for 3rd row, sl 1, k2 for 4th row.

5th and 6th turning rows: K3, sl 1, turn, for 5th row, sl 1, k3 for 6th row.

7th and 8th turning rows: K2, sl 1, turn, for 7th row, sl 1, k2 for 8th row.

9th and 10th turning rows: K1, sl 1, turn, for 9th row, sl 1, k1 for 10th row, turn.

Next row: K4, m1, k last 3 sts, m1, k3.

Next row: P to last 4 sts, sl last 4 sts on to a safety-pin.

1st row: K1, sl 1, k1, psso, k to end.

2nd row: P to last 3 sts, p2tog tbl, p1.

3rd row: K1, sl 1, k1, psso, k to end.

4th row: P to last 3 sts, p2tog tbl, p1.

5th row: K1, sl 1, k1, psso, k to last 3 sts, m1, k3.

6th row: P to last 3 sts, p2tog tbl, p1.

Rep last 6 rows, 4 times more, then work the 1st to 5th rows again. 79(86:93) sts.

Work 2(4:8) rows, dec at neck edge on every row as before.

Shape armhole and cont to shape neck.

Next row: Cast off 5 sts, p to last 3 sts, p2tog tbl, p1.

Next row: K1, sl 1, k1, psso, k to end.

Next row: Cast off 4 sts, p to last 3 sts, p2tog tbl, p1.

Next row: K1, sl 1, k1, psso, k to last 5 sts, k2tog, k3.

Next row: P to last 3 sts, p2tog tbl, p1.

Work as left front from *** to end.

SLEEVES

With 2¾mm (No 12/US 2) needles, cast on 64(66:68) sts.

K9 rows.

Change to 3¼mm (No 10/US 3) needles.

Beg with a k row, work 2 rows in st st.

Inc row: K3, m1, k to last 3 sts, m1, k1. 66(68:70) sts.

Work 11(9:7) rows.

Rep last 12(10:8) rows, 11(13:15) times more. 90(96:102) sts.

Cont in st st until work measures 44cm/17¼in from beg, ending with a p row.

Shape sleeve top

Cast off 5 sts at beg of next 2 rows and 4 sts on foll 2 rows.

Next row: K3, sl 1, k1, psso, k to last 5 sts, k2tog, k3.

Next row: P to end.

Rep last 2 rows, 9(10:11) times. 52(56:60) sts.

Cast off.

RIGHT HALF EDGING AND COLLAR

Join shoulder seams. Place right front over left front and place a marker where each front crosses. With wrong side of right front facing, using 2¾mm (No 12/US 2) needles, rejoin yarn to inner edge of sts on safety-pin and k to end.

Cont in gst until edging fits up front to marker, ending at front edge.

Cont in gst, inc 1 st at inner edge for collar on the next row and the 26 foll alt rows. 31 sts.

Cont in gst until border and collar fits up right front to shoulder, ending at outer edge.

Shape collar

1st and 2nd turning rows: K17, turn, for 1st row, sl 1, k to end for 2nd row.

K6 rows.

Rep last 8 rows, until inner edge fits across to centre back neck.

Cast off.

LEFT HALF EDGING AND COLLAR

With right side of left front facing, using 2¾mm (No 12/US 2) needles, rejoin yarn to inner edge of sts on safety-pin and work as given for right half edging and collar.

TIES (make 2)

With 2¾mm (No 12/US 2) needles, cast on 5 sts.

Work in gst for 56(62:68)cm/22(24½:26¾)in.

Cast off.

TO MAKE UP

Set sleeves into armholes. Sew ties to fronts at beg of front shaping. Join side and sleeve seams, leaving a small opening in right seam, having opening level with tie at front edge. Sew edging and collar to front edge and across to centre back neck. Join centre back seam of collar.

Lace and Cable Tunic

MATERIALS
24 x 50g balls of Rowan Denim.
Pair each of 3¼mm (No 10/US 3) and 4mm (No 8/US 6) knitting needles.

MEASUREMENTS

To fit chest size	81cm	
	32in	
Actual measurement	108cm	
	42½in	
Length	58cm	
	22¾in	
Sleeve seam	32cm	
	12½in	

TENSION BEFORE WASHING
See basic information on page 7.
20 sts and 28 rows to 10cm/4in square over st st on 4mm (No 8/US 6) needles.

ABBREVIATIONS
C4 or 6B = Sl next 2 or 3 sts on to a cable needle and leave at back, k2 or 3, then k2 or 3 from cable needle.
C4 or 6F = Sl next 2 or 3 sts on to cable needle and leave at front, k2 or 3, then k2 or 3 from cable needle.
T5B = Sl next 2 sts on to cable needle and leave at back, k3, then p2 from cable needle.
T5F = Sl next 3 sts on to cable needle and leave at front, p2, then k3 from cable needle.
Cr3L = Sl next 2 sts on to cable needle and leave at front, p1, then k2 from cable needle.
Cr3R = Sl next st on to cable needle and leave at back, k2, then p st from cable needle.
Cr2L = Sl next st on to cable needle and leave at front, p1, then k st from cable needle.
Cr2R = Sl next st on to cable needle and leave at back, k1, then p st from cable needle.
Also see page 7.

PATTERN PANEL A (worked over 35 sts)
1st row (wrong side): K2, [p6, k4] 3 times, p3.
2nd row: K3, [p4, C6F] 3 times, p2.
3rd row: K2, [p6, k4] 3 times, p3.
4th row: [T5F, T5B] 3 times, T5F.
5th row: P3, [k4, p6] 3 times, k2.
6th row: P2, [C6B, p4] 3 times, k3.
7th row: P3, [k4, p6] 3 times, k2.
8th row: [T5B, T5F] 3 times, T5B.
These 8 rows form the patt for panel A.

PATTERN PANEL B (worked over 8 sts)
1st row (wrong side): K2, p4, k2.
2nd row: P2, k4, p2.
3rd row: K2, p4, k2.
4th row: P2, C4F, p2.
These 4 rows form the patt for panel B.

PATTERN PANEL C (worked over 11 sts)
1st and every alternate row (wrong side): P11.
2nd row: K6, sl 1, k1, psso, yf, k3.
4th row: K5, sl 1, k1, psso, yf, k4.
6th row: K4, sl 1, k1, psso, yf, k5.
8th row: K3, sl 1, k1, psso, yf, k6.
10th row: K2, sl 1, k1, psso, yf, k7.
12th row: K3, yf, k2tog, k6.
14th row: K4, yf, k2tog, k5.
16th row: K5, yf, k2tog, k4.
18th row: K6, yf, k2tog, k3.
20th row: K7, yf, k2tog, k2.
These 20 rows form the patt for panel C.

PATTERN PANEL D (worked over 14 sts)
1st row (wrong side): K2, [p4, k2] twice.
2nd row: P2, [C4B, p2] twice.
3rd row: K2, [p4, k2] twice.
4th row: P2, k2, Cr3L, Cr3R, k2, p2.
5th row: K2, p2, k1, p4, k1, p2, k2.
6th row: P2, k2, p1, C4F, p1, k2, p2.
7th row: K2, p2, k1, p4, k1, p2, k2.
8th row: P2, k2, Cr3R, Cr3L, k2, p2.
These 8 rows form the patt for panel D.

PATTERN PANEL E (worked over 11 sts)

1st and every alternate row (wrong side): P11.

2nd row: K5, yf, sl 1, k1, psso, k4.

4th row: K3, k2tog, yf, k1, yf, sl 1, k1, psso, k3.

6th row: K2, k2tog, yf, k3, yf, sl 1, k1, psso, k2.

8th row: K1, k2tog, yf, k5, yf, sl 1, k1, psso, k1.

10th row: K11.

These 10 rows form the patt for panel E.

BACK

With 3¼mm (No 10/US 3) needles, cast on 129 sts.

1st row (wrong side): P3, * k4, p1, k4, p3 *;

work from * to * twice more, work across 1st row of patt panels B, A and B, p3, ** k4, p1, k4, p3; work from ** twice more.

2nd row: K3, * p2, Cr2R, k1, Cr2L, p2, k3 *; work from * to * twice more, work across 2nd row of pattern panels B, A and B, k3, ** p2, Cr2R, k1, Cr2L, p2, k3; work from ** twice more.

3rd row: P3, * k2, p1, [k1, p1] twice, k2, p3 *;

work from * to * twice more, work across 3rd row of patt panels B, A and B, p3, ** k2, p1, [k1, p1] twice, k2, p3; work from ** twice more.

4th row: K3, * p1, Cr2R, p1, k1, p1, Cr2L, p1, k3 *; work from * to * twice more, work across 4th row of patt panels B, A and B, k3, ** p1, Cr2R, p1, k1, p1, Cr2L, p1, k3; work from ** twice more.

The last 4 rows form the patt for panel B and set position of patt for panel A.

5th row: P3, * k1, p1, [k2, p1] twice, k1, p3 *; work from * to * twice more, panel patt 51, p3, ** k1, p1, [k2, p1] twice, k1, p3; work from ** twice more.

6th row: K3, * Cr2R, p2, k1, p2, Cr2L, k3 *; work from * to * twice more, panel patt 51, k3, ** Cr2R, p2, k1, p2, Cr2L, k3; work from ** twice more.

These 6 rows form the patt for the welt. ***

Cont in patt as set until 59 rows have been completed.

**** Inc row: Patt 7, [m1, patt 7] 4 times, m1, patt 59, m1, [patt 7, m1] 4 times, patt 7. 139 sts.

Change to 4mm (No 8/US 6) needles and work main patt thus:

1st row (wrong side): Work across 1st row of patt panels B, C, D, E and B, work across 5th row of patt panel A, work across 1st row of patt panels B, E, D, C and B.

2nd row: Work across 2nd row of patt panels B, C, D, E and B, work across 6th row of patt panel A, work across 2nd row of patt panels B, E, D, C, and B.

3rd row: Work across 3rd row of patt panels B, C, D, E and B, work across 7th row of patt panel A, work across 3rd row of patt panels B, E, D, C and B.

4th row: Work across 4th row of patt panels B, C, D, E and B, work across the 8th row of patt panel A, work across 4th row of patt panels B, E, D, C and B.

These 4 rows set the patt panels.

Cont in patt until work measures 62cm/24¼in from beg, ending with a wrong side row.

Shape shoulders

Cast off 25 sts at beg of next 4 rows.

Leave rem 39 sts on a spare needle.

POCKET LININGS (make 2)

With 4mm (No 8/US 6) needles, cast on 24 sts.

Beg with a k row, work 41 rows in st st, inc 3 sts evenly across the last row. 27 sts. Leave these sts on a st holder.

FRONT

Work as back to ***.

Cont in patt as set until 54 rows have been completed.

1st pocket row: Patt 6, cast off 27 sts, patt to last 33 sts, cast off next 27 sts, patt to end.

2nd pocket row: Patt 6, patt across the 27 sts of one pocket lining, patt to last 6 sts, patt across the 27 sts of other pocket lining, patt 6. 129 sts.

Cont in patt for a further 3 rows.

Work as back from **** to end.

SLEEVES

With 3¼mm (No 10/US 3) needles, cast on 59 sts.

1st row: K1, p2, Cr2R, k1, Cr2L, p2,* k3, p2, Cr2R, k1, Cr2L, p2; work from * to last st, k1.

2nd row: P1, k2, p1, [k1, p1] twice, k2, * p3, k2, p1, [k1, p1] twice, k2; work from * to last st, p1.

These 2 rows set position of the welt patt for the cuff.

Cont in welt patt to match back for a further 15 rows, inc 2 sts evenly across last row. 61 sts.

Change to 4mm (No 8/US 6) needles.

1st row (wrong side): P5, work across 1st row of patt panels B, A and B, p5.

2nd row: K5, work across 2nd row of patt panels B, A and B, k5.

3rd row: P5, work across 3rd row of patt panels B, A and B, p5.

4th row: K5, work across 4th row of patt panels B, A and B, k5.

These 4 rows set position of the patt panels.

Cont in patt, taking extra sts into panel E, then panel B as they occur, inc 1 st each end of the next row and the 11 foll 5th rows. 85 sts.

Cont until work measures 40cm/15¾in from beg, ending with a wrong side row.

Cast off 23 sts at beg of next 2 rows. 39 sts.

Saddle shoulder extension

Cont on rem sts for 18cm/7in, ending with a wrong side row.

Shape neck edge

Next row: Patt 9, work 2tog, turn.

Dec 1 st at inner edge on each of the next 8 rows. 2 sts.

Work 2tog and fasten off.

With right side facing, rejoin yarn to inner edge of rem 28 sts, cast off 17, work 2tog, patt to end.

Dec 1 st at inner edge on each of the next 8 rows. 2 sts.

Work 2tog and fasten off.

NECKBAND
Join saddle shoulders leaving left back free. With right side facing, using 3¼mm (No 10/US 3) needles, pick up and k29 sts around shaped edge of left sleeve saddle shoulder extension, k the 39 sts at centre front, pick up and k28 sts around shaped edge of right sleeve saddle shoulder extension, then k39 sts at centre back. 135 sts.
1st row: K3, [p3, k3] to end.
2nd row: P3, [k3, p3] to end.
Rep last 2 rows 5 times more, then work the 1st row again.
Change to 4mm (No 8/US 6) needles.

Next row: P3, [k4, p1, k4, p3] to end.
Beg with the 2nd row, work 16 rows in patt as given for welt on each side of centre panels on back.
Cast off loosely in pattern.

TO MAKE UP
First, see basic information on page 7. Then mark side edges, 11.5cm/4½in down from shoulders. Join left back saddle shoulder and neckband, reversing seam on neckband to allow for fold back. Sew cast-off sts at top of sleeves to row-ends on back and front. Join side and sleeve seams. Catch pocket linings to wrong side.

Moss Stitch Denim Jacket

MATERIALS
5(6:7) 50g balls of Rowan Denim.
Pair each of 3¼mm (No 10/US 3) and 4mm (No 8/US 6) knitting needles.
5(6:7) buttons.

MEASUREMENTS

To fit ages	3-6	6-9	9-12 months
Actual chest measurement	58.5	66.5	73.5cm
	23	26¼	29in
Length	25	30	33cm
	10	12	13in
Sleeve seam with cuff turned back	15	19	21cm
	6	7½	8½in

TENSION BEFORE WASHING
See basic information on page 7.
20 sts and 30 rows to 10cm/4in square over mst on 4mm (No 8 /US 6) needles.

ABBREVIATIONS
See page 7.

BACK
With 3¼mm (No 10/US 3) needles, cast on 57(65:71) sts.
Gst, (every row k), 7(7:9) rows.
Change to 4mm (No 8/US 6) needles.
Mst row (right side): K1, [p1, k1] to end.
Work in mst until back measures 32(37:41)cm/12½(14½:16)in from beg, ending with a wrong side row.
Shape shoulders
Cast off 8(10:10) sts at beg of next 2 rows and 9(10:11) sts at beg of foll 2 rows.
Cast off rem 23(25:29) sts.

POCKET LININGS (make 2)
With 4mm (No 8/US 6) needles, cast on 21(23:25) sts.
Work 29(31:33) rows in mst as given for back.
Leave sts on a st holder.

LEFT FRONT
With 3¼mm (No 10/US 3) needles, cast on 33(37:41) sts.
Gst 7(7:9) rows.
Change to 4mm (No 8/US 6) needles.
1st row (right side): [K1, p1] 14(16:18) times, k5.
2nd row: K5, [p1, k1] 14(16:18) times.
Rep last 2 rows until work measures 12(14:16)cm/4¾(5½:6¼)in from beg, ending with a wrong side row.
1st pocket row: Mst 6(8:10), then mst 21(23:25) and leave these sts on a st holder, mst 1, k5.
2nd pocket row: K5, mst 1, mst across the 21(23:25) sts of one pocket lining, mst to end. 33(37:41) sts.
Keeping 5 sts at front edge in gst, cont in patt until work measures 25(30:33)cm/9¾(11¾:13)in from beg, ending with a wrong side row.
Shape neck
Next row: Pattern to last 8(9:10) sts, turn and leave these sts on a safety-pin.
** Dec 1 st at neck edge on each of the next 8(8:10) rows. 17 (20:21) sts.
Cont in patt until work measures the same as back to shoulder, ending at side edge.
Shape shoulder
Cast off 8(10:10) sts at beg of next row.
Work 1 row.
Cast off rem 9(10:11) sts.

RIGHT FRONT
With 3¼mm (No 10/US 3) needles, cast on 33(37:41) sts.
Gst 5 rows.
Buttonhole row: K3, yf, k2tog, k to end.
Mark positions for a further 4(5:6) buttons along left front, placing markers so that they are evenly spaced, having the last marker 1cm/½in down from neck edge.
Working buttonholes to correspond with markers, cont thus:
Gst 1(1:3) rows.
Change to 4mm (No 8/US 6) needles.
1st row (right side): K5, [p1, k1] to end.
2nd row: [k1, p1] to last 5 sts, k5.
Rep last 2 rows until work measures 12(14:16)cm/4¾(5½:6¼)in from beg, ending with a wrong side row.
1st pocket row: K5, mst 1, patt 21(23:25) and leave these sts on a st holder, mst 6(8:10).
2nd pocket row: Mst 6(8:10), patt across the 21(23:25) sts of other pocket lining, mst 1, k5. 33 (37:41) sts.
Keeping 5 sts at front edge in gst, cont in mst until work measures 25(30:33)cm/9¾(11¾:13)in, ending with a wrong side row.
Shape neck
Next row: Mst 8 (9:10) and leave these sts on a safety-pin, mst to end.
Work as left front from ** to end.

SLEEVES
With 3¼mm (No 10/US 3) needles, cast on 32(36:42) sts.
Work in gst for 5(5:6)cm/2(2:2¼)in.
Change to 4mm (No 8/US 6) needles.
1st mst row (right side): [K1, p1] to end.
2nd mst row: [P1, k1] to end.
Rep last 2 rows, once more.
Keeping continuity of mst, inc 1 st each end of next row and the 6(8:8) foll 4th rows. 46(54:60) sts.
Cont in mst until sleeve measures 21(26:30)cm/8¼(10¼:11¾)in

from beg, ending with a wrong side row.
Cast off.

COLLAR

Join shoulder seams. With right side facing, using 3¼mm (No 10/US 3) needles, sl 8(9:10) sts from right front safety-pin on to needle, pick up and k14(14:16) sts up right front neck, 23(25:29) sts across back neck and 14(14:16) sts down left front neck, then k the 8(9:10) sts from left front safety-pin. 67(71:81) sts.
Gst 1 row.
Cont in gst, cast off 3 sts at beg of next 2 rows. 61 (65:75) sts.
1st turning row: K48(51:58), turn.
2nd row: K35(37:41), turn.
3rd row: K41(43:47), turn.
4th row: K47(49:53), turn
5th row: K53(55:59), turn.
6th row: K59(61:65), turn.
Next row: K to end of row.

Next row: K2, m1, k to last 2 sts, m1, k2. 63(67:77) sts.
K5 rows.
Rep last 6 rows, twice more. 67(71:81) sts.
Cast off.

POCKET TOPS

With wrong side facing, using 3¼mm (No 10/US 3) needles, k across the 21(23:25) sts on st holder.
K3 rows.
Cast off kwise.

TO MAKE UP

First, see basic information on page 7. Then mark side edges on back and front, 11(13.5:15)cm/4½(5¼:6)in down from shoulder. Sew cast-off edge of sleeves to row-ends above markers on back and fronts. Join side and sleeve seams. Sew pocket linings to wrong side and row-ends of pocket tops to right side. Add buttons.

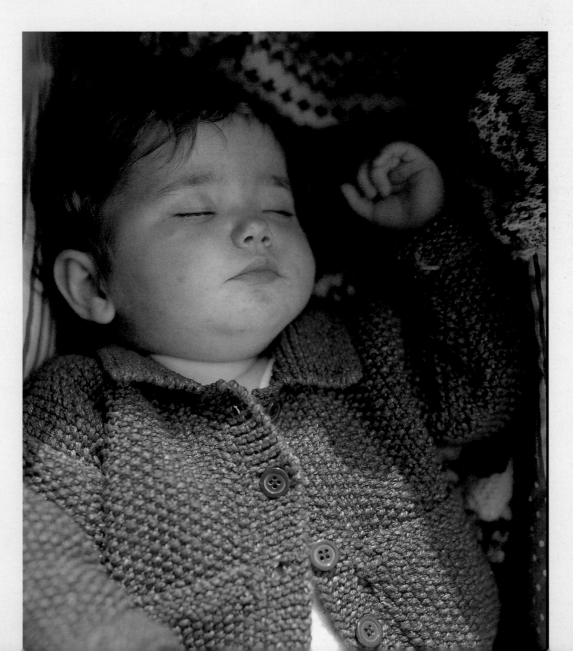

Cabled Tweed Jacket

MATERIALS

12(14) 50g hanks of Rowan DK Tweed.
Pair each of 3¼mm (No 10/US 3), 3¾mm (No 9/US 4) and 4mm
(No 8/US 6) knitting needles.
A cable needle.
5 buttons.

MEASUREMENTS

To fit bust sizes	86	91cm
	34	36in
Actual measurement	95.5	104.5cm
	37½	41½in
Length	54	55.5cm
	21	21¾in
Sleeve seam	44.5	44.5cm
	17½	17½in

TENSION

27 sts and 31 rows to 10cm/4in square over patt on 4mm
(No 8/US 6) needles.

ABBREVIATIONS

C4F = Sl next 2 sts on to cable needle and leave at front of
work, k2, then k2 from cable needle.
See also page 7.

RIGHT HALF BACK OPENING

With 3¾mm (No 9/US 4) needles, cast on 57(63) sts.
Mst row: K1, [p1, k1] to end.
Rep last row, 6 times more.
Inc row (wrong side): [K1, p1] 3 times, * p1, m1, p2, k6(7); rep
from * to last 6(7) sts, p1, m1, p2, k3(4). 63(69) sts.
Change to 4mm (No 8/US 6) needles and work in patt.
1st row: P3(4), *k4, p6(7); rep from * to last 10 sts, k4, [p1, k1] 3
times.
2nd row: [K1, p1] 3 times, * p4, k6(7); rep from * to last 7(8) sts,
p4, k3(4).
3rd row: P3(4), * k4, p6(7); rep from * to last 10 sts, k4, [p1, k1] 3
times.
4th row: [K1, p1] 3 times, * p4, k6(7); rep from * to last 7(8) sts,
p4, k3(4).
5th row: P3(4), * C4F, p6(7); rep from * to last 10 sts, C4F, [p1,
k1] 3 times.
6th row: [K1, p1] 3 times, * p4, k6(7); rep from * to last 7(8) sts,
p4, k3(4).
These 6 rows form the cable patt with mst border.
Patt a further 22 rows.
Next row: Patt to last 6(5) sts, cast off 6(5).
Leave rem 57(64) sts on a spare needle.

LEFT HALF BACK OPENING

With 3¾mm (No 9/US 4) needles, cast on 57(63) sts.
Mst row: K1, [p1, k1] to end.
Rep last row, 6 times more.
Inc row (wrong side): K3(4), * p1, m1, p2, k6(7); rep from * to last
9 sts, p1, m1, p2, [p1, k1] 3 times. 63(69) sts.
Change to 4mm (No 8/US 6) needles and work in patt.
1st row: [K1, p1] 3 times, * k4, p6(7); rep from * to last 7(8) sts,
k4, p3(4).
2nd row: K3(4), * p4, k6(7); rep from * to last 10 sts, p4, [p1, k1] 3
times.
3rd row: [K1, p1] 3 times, * k4, p6(7); rep from * to last 7(8) sts,
k4, p3(4).
4th row: K3(4), * p4, k6(7); rep from * to last 10 sts, p4, [p1, k1] 3
times.
5th row: [K1, p1] 3 times, * C4F, p6(7); rep from * to last 7(8) sts,
C4F, p3(4).
6th row: K3(4), * p4, k6(7); rep from * to last 10 sts, p4, [p1, k1] 3
times.
These 6 rows form the cable patt with mst border.
Patt a further 23 rows.
30th joining row: Work across left half back opening thus: Patt to
last 6 sts, k6, then k0(1), from 57(64) sts of right back opening,
patt to end. 120(133) sts.
1st dec row: P3(4), * k4, p2(3), p2tog, p2; rep from * to last 7(8)
sts, k4, p3(4). 109(122) sts.
Patt 5 rows.
2nd dec row: P3(4), * k4, p1(2), p2tog, p2; rep from * to last 7(8)
sts, k4, p3(4). 98(111) sts.
Patt 5 rows.
3rd dec row: P3(4), * k4, p1(2), p2tog, p1; rep from * to last 7(8)
sts, k4, p3(4). 87(100) sts.
Patt 5 rows.
4th dec row: P3(4) , * k4, p2tog, p1(2); rep from * to last 7(8) sts,
k4, p3(4). 76(89) sts.
Patt 5 rows.
1st inc row: P3(4), * k4, p1(2), m1, p1; rep from * to last 7(8) sts,
k4, p3(4). 87(100) sts.
Patt 5 rows.
2nd inc row: P1(2), m1, p2, * k4, p2, m1, p1(2); rep from * to last
7(8) sts, k4, p2, m1, p1(2). 100(113) sts.
Patt 5 rows.
3rd inc row: P4(5), * k4, p2, m1, p2(3) ; rep from * to last 8(9) sts,
k4, p4(5). 111(124) sts.
Patt 5 rows.
4th inc row: P1(2), m1, p3, * k4, p2, m1, p3(4); rep from * to last
8(9) sts, k4, p3, m1, p1(2). 124(137) sts.
Patt 5 rows.
5th inc row: P1(2), m1, p4, * k4, p6(7); rep from * to last 9(10) sts,
k4, p4, m1, p1(2). 126(139) sts.
Cont in patt for a further 23 rows.

Shape armholes

Cast off 6(8) sts at beg of next 2 rows and 2 sts at beg of foll 4 rows.

Dec 1 st each end of next row and on the 2 foll alt rows. 100(109) sts.

Patt a further 43(47) rows.

Shape shoulders

Cast off 11(12) sts at beg of next 6 rows.

Cast off rem 34(37) sts.

LEFT FRONT

With 3¾mm (No 9/US 4) needles, cast on 57(63) sts.

Mst row: K1, [p1, k1] to end.

Rep last row, 6 times more.

Inc row (wrong side): [K1, p1] 3 times, * p1, m1, p2, k6(7); rep from * to last 6(7) sts, p1, m1, p2, k3(4). 63(69) sts.

Change to 4mm (No 8/US 6) needles and work in patt.

1st row: P3(4), * k4, p6(7); rep from * to last 10 sts, k4, [p1, k1] 3 times.

2nd row: [K1, p1] 3 times, * p4, k6(7); rep from * to last 7(8) sts, p4, k3(4).

3rd row: P3(4), * k4, p6(7); rep from * to last 10 sts, k4, [p1, k1] 3 times.

4th row: [K1, p1] 3 times, * p4, k6(7); rep from * to last 7(8) sts, p4, k3(4).

5th row: P3(4), C4F, p6(7); rep from * to last 10 sts, C4F, [p1, k1]

3 times.

6th row: [K1, p1] 3 times, * p4, k6(7); rep from * to last 7(8) sts, p4, k3(4).

These 6 rows form the cable patt with mst border.

Patt a further 24 rows.

1st dec row: P3(4), * k4, p2(3), p2tog, p2; rep from * to last 10 sts, k4, mst 6. 58(64) sts.

Patt 5 rows.

2nd dec row: P3(4), * k4, p1(2), p2tog, p2; rep from * to last 10 sts, k4, mst 6. 53(59) sts.

Patt 5 rows.

3rd dec row: P3(4), * k4, p1(2), p2tog, p1; rep from * to last 10 sts, k4, mst 6. 48(54) sts.

Patt 5 rows.

4th dec row: P3(4), * k4, p2tog, p1(2); rep from * to last 10 sts, k4, mst 6. 43(49) sts.

Patt 5 rows.

1st inc row: P3(4), * k4, p1(2), m1, p1; rep from * to last 10 sts, k4, mst 6. 48(54) sts.

Patt 5 rows.

2nd inc row: P1(2), m1, p2, * k4, p2, m1, p1(2); rep from * to last 10 sts, k4, mst 6. 54(60) sts.

Patt 5 rows.

3rd inc row: P4(5), * k4, p2, m1, p2(3); rep from * to last 10 sts, k4, mst 6. 59(65) sts.

Patt 5 rows.

4th inc row: P1(2), m1, p3, * k4, p2, m1, p3(4); rep from * to last 10 sts, k4, mst 6. 65(71) sts.

Patt 5 rows straight.

5th inc row: P1(2), m1, p4, k4, p6(7), rep from * to last 10 sts, k4, mst 6. 66(72) sts.

Cont in patt for a further 23 rows.

Shape armhole

Cast off 6(8) sts at beg of next row.

Patt 1 row.

Cast off 2 sts at beg of next and foll alt row.

Dec 1 st at armhole edge on next and 2 foll alt rows. 53(57) sts.

Patt a further 14 rows.

Shape neck

Next row: Patt 6 and leave on a safety-pin, patt to end.

** Dec 1 st at neck edge on next row and the 13(14) foll alt rows. 33(36) sts.

Patt 1(3) row(s).

Shape shoulder

Cast off 11(12) sts at beg of next and foll alt row. 11(12) sts.

Patt 1 row.

Cast off.

RIGHT FRONT

With 3¾mm (No 9/US 5) needles, cast on 57(63) sts.

Mst row: K1, [p1, k1] to end.

Rep last row, 6 times more.

Inc row (wrong side): K3(4), * p1, m1, p2, k6(7); rep from * to last

9 sts, p1, m1, p2, [p1, k1] 3 times. 63(69) sts.

Change to 4mm (No 8/US 6) needles and work in patt.

1st row: [K1, p1] 3 times, * k4, p6(7); rep from * to last 7(8) sts, k4, p3(4).

2nd row: K3(4), * p4, k6(7); rep from * to last 10 sts, p4, [k1, p1] 3 times.

3rd row: [K1, p1] 3 times, * k4, p6(7); rep from * to last 7(8) sts, k4, p3(4).

4th row: K3(4), * p4, k6(7); rep from * to last 10 sts, p4, [p1, k1] 3 times.

5th row: [K1, p1] 3 times, * C4F, p6(7); rep from * to last 7(8) sts, C4F, p3(4).

6th row: K3(4), * p4, k6(7); rep from * to last 10 sts, p4, [p1, k1] 3 times.

These 6 rows form the cable patt with mst border.

Patt 18 rows.

Buttonhole row: K1, p1, k2tog, yf, k1, p1, patt to end.

Patt 5 rows.

1st dec row: Mst 6, k4, * p2, p2tog, p2(3), k4; rep from * to last 3(4) sts, p to end. 58(64) sts.

Patt 5 rows.

2nd dec row: Mst 6, k4, * p2, p2tog, p1(2), k4; rep from * to last 3(4) sts, p to end. 53(59) sts.

Patt 5 rows.

3rd dec row: Mst 6, k4, * p1, p2tog, p1(2), k4; rep from * to last 3(4) sts, p to end. 48(54) sts.

Patt 5 rows.

4th dec and buttonhole row: K1, p1, k2tog, yf, k1, p1, k4, * p1(2), p2tog, k4; rep from * to last 3(4) sts, p to end. 43(49) sts.

Patt 5 rows.

1st inc row: Mst 6, k4, * p1, m1, p1(2), k4; rep from * to last 3(4) sts, p to end. 48(54) sts.

Patt 5 rows.

2nd inc row: Mst 6, k4, * p1(2), m1, p2, k4; rep from * to last 3(4) sts, p2, m1, p1(2). 54(60) sts.

Patt 5 rows.

3rd inc row: Mst 6, k4, * p2(3), m1, p2, k4; rep from * to last 4(5) sts, p to end. 59(65) sts.

Patt 5 rows.

4th inc and buttonhole row: K1, p1, k2tog, yf, k1, p1, k4, * p3(4), m1, p2, k4; rep from * to last 4(5) sts, p3, m1, p1(2). 65(71) sts.

Patt 5 rows.

5th inc row: Mst 6, k4, * p6(7) , k4; rep from * to last 5(6) sts, p4, m1, p1(2). 66(72) sts.

Cont in patt for a further 17 rows.

Buttonhole row: K1, p1, k2tog, yf, k1, p1, patt to end.

Patt 6 rows.

Shape armhole

Next row: Cast off 6(8) sts, patt to end.

Patt 1 row.

Cast off 2 sts at beg of next and foll alt row.

Dec 1 st at armhole edge on next and 2 foll alt rows. 53(57) sts.

Patt 7 rows.

Buttonhole row: K1, p1, k2tog, yf, k1, p1, patt to end.
Patt 7 rows.
Shape neck
Next row: Patt 5, inc, and leave these 7 sts on a safety-pin, patt to end.
Work as left front from ** to end.

SLEEVES

With 3¾mm (No 9/US 5) needles, cast on 51(55) sts.
Work 11 rows in mst as given for left front.
Inc row (wrong side): Mst 6(5), * m1, mst 5; rep from * to end. 60(65) sts.
Change to 4mm (No 8/US 6) needles and work in patt.
1st row: P3, * k4, p6(7); rep from * to last 7 sts, k4, p3.
2nd row: K3, * p4, k6(7); rep from * to last 7 sts, p4, k3.
3rd row: As 1st row.
4th row: As 2nd row.
5th row: P3, * C4F, p6(7); rep from * to last 7 sts, C4F, p3.
6th row: As 2nd row.
These 6 rows form patt for the sleeves.
Keeping continuity of patt, taking extra sts into patt as they occur, inc 1 st each end of next row and the 13 foll 8th rows. 88(93) sts.
Patt 17 rows.
Shape top
Cast off 6(8) sts at beg of next 2 rows.
Dec 1 st each end of next 6(3) rows.
Work 0(3) rows, dec 0(1) st each end of 2nd of these rows.
Cast off 3 sts at beg of next 4 rows. 52(57) sts.
Cast off.

LEFT HALF COLLAR

First join shoulder seam.
With right side facing, using 3¼mm (No 10/US 3) needles, rejoin yarn to inner edge of 6 sts on left front safety-pin.
1st inc row: Inc, mst 5. 7 sts.
2nd (right side) row: Mst 6, k1.
3rd inc row: Inc pwise, Mst 6. 8 sts.
4th row: Mst 6, k2.
5th inc row: Inc pwise, p1, mst 6. 9 sts.
6th row: Mst 6, k3.
7th inc row: Inc pwise, p2, mst 6. 10 sts.
8th row: Mst 6, k4.
9th inc row: Inc pwise, p3, mst 6. 11 sts.
10th row: Mst 6, C4F, p1.
11th inc row: Inc kwise, p4, mst 6. 12 sts.
12th row: Mst 6, k4, p2.
13th inc row: Inc kwise, k1, p4, mst 6. 13 sts
14th row: Mst 6, k4, p3.
*** Keeping continuity of mst and 6-row cable, taking extra sts into reverse st st as they occur, inc 1 st at inner edge on the next row and the 6 foll alt rows. 20 sts.
Cont in patt until left half collar fits up shaped edge of neck to shoulder, ending at outer edge.

Shape collar
1st and 2nd turning rows: Patt 12, turn, patt to end.
Patt 4 rows.
Rep last 6 rows until inner edge of collar fits across to centre back neck.
Cast off.

RIGHT HALF COLLAR

With wrong side facing, using 3¼ mm (No10/ US 3) needles, rejoin yarn to inner edge of 7 sts on right front safety-pin.
1st row (right side): K1, mst 6.
2nd inc row: Mst 6, inc pwise. 8 sts.
3rd row: K2, mst 6.
4th inc row: Mst 6, p1, inc pwise. 9 sts.
5th row: K3, mst 6.
6th inc row: Mst 6, p2, inc pwise. 10 sts.
7th row: K4, mst 6.
8th inc row: Mst 6, p3, inc pwise. 11 sts.
9th row: P1, C4F, mst 6.
10th inc row: Mst 6, p4, inc kwise. 12 sts.
11th row: P2, k4, mst 6.
12th inc row: Mst 6, p4, k1, inc kwise. 13 sts.
13th row: P3, k4, mst 6.
Work as left half collar from *** to end.

TO MAKE UP

Set in sleeves. Join side and sleeve seams. Sew shaped edge of collar to neck edge and across to centre back neck. Join cast-off edges tog. Sew on buttons. Catch down cast off stitches at top of back opening on wrong side.

Shaped Denim Jacket

MATERIALS
17(19) 50g balls of Rowan Denim.
Pair each of 3¾mm (No 9/US 4) and 4mm (No 8/US 6) knitting needles.
A cable needle.
7 buttons.

MEASUREMENTS

To fit bust sizes	86	91cm
	34	36in
Actual measurement	103	107cm
	40½	42in
Length	57	58.5cm
	22½	23in
Sleeve seam	42.5	42.5cm
	16¾	16¾in

TENSION BEFORE WASHING
See basic information on page 7.
20 sts and 30 rows, to 10cm/4in square over patt on 4mm (No 8/US 6) needles.

ABBREVIATIONS
Tw5 = Sl next 2 sts onto cable needle and leave at front, k2, p1, then k2 from cable needle.
Tw3B = Sl next st on to cable needle and leave at back, k2, then p st from cable needle.
Tw3F = Sl next 2 sts on to cable needle and leave at front, p1, k2 from cable needle.
See also page 7.

PATTERN PANEL (worked over 17(19) sts)
1st row: P6(7), Tw5, p6(7).
2nd row: K6(7), p2, k1, p2, k6(7).
3rd row: P5(6), Tw3B, k1, Tw3F, p5(6).
4th row: K5(6), p2, k1, p1, k1, p2, k5(6).
5th row: P4(5), Tw3B, k1, p1, k1, Tw3F, p4(5).
6th row: K4(5), p2, [k1, p1] twice, k1, p2, k4(5).
7th row: P3(4), Tw3B, [k1, p1] twice, k1, Tw3F, p3(4).
8th row: K3(4), p2, [k1, p1] 3 times, k1, p2, k3(4).
9th row: P2(3), Tw3B, [k1, p1] 3 times, k1, Tw3F, p2(3).
10th row: K2(3), p2, [k1, p1] 4 times, k1, p2, k2(3).
11th row: P1(2), Tw3B, [k1, p1] 4 times, k1, Tw3F, p1(2).
12th row: K1(2), p2, [k1, p1] 5 times, k1, p2, k1(2).
These 12 rows form the patt panel.

BACK
With 3¾mm (No 9/US 4) needles, cast on 109 (117) sts.
Mst row (right side): K1, [p1, k1] to end.
Mst a further 6 rows.

Inc row: Mst 17(18), [m1, mst 25(27)] 3 times, m1, mst 17(18). 113(121) sts.
Change to 4mm (No 8/US 6) needles.
Work in patt thus:
1st row: Mst 9 [work 1st row of patt panel, mst 9] 4 times.
2nd row: Mst 9, [work 2nd row of patt panel, mst 9] 4 times.
These 2 rows set the position of the patt.
Cont in patt as set for a further 20 rows.
1st dec row: Mst 7, [work 2tog, patt 17(19), work 2tog, mst 5] 3 times, work 2tog, patt 17(19), work 2tog, mst 7. 105(113) sts.
Patt another 11 rows.
2nd dec row: Mst 6, [work 2tog, patt 17(19), work 2tog, mst 3] 3 times, work 2tog, patt 17(19), work 2tog, mst 6. 97(105) sts.
Patt another 17 rows.
3rd dec row: Mst 5, [work 2tog, patt 17(19), work 2tog, mst 1] 3 times, work 2tog, patt 17(19), work 2tog, mst 5. 89(97) sts.
Patt another 23 rows.
1st inc row: Mst 6, [m1, patt 17(19), m1, mst 3] 3 times, m1, patt 17(19), m1, mst 6. 97 (105) sts.
Patt another 17 rows.
2nd inc row: Mst 7, [m1, patt 17(19), m1, mst 5] 3 times, m1, patt 17(19), m1, mst 7. 105(113) sts.
Patt another 11 rows.
3rd inc row: Mst 8, [m1, patt 17(19), m1, mst 7] 3 times, m1, patt 17(19), m1, mst 8. 113(121) sts. Patt another 15 rows.

Shape armholes
Cast off 4 sts at beg of next 2 rows.
Dec 1 st each end of next row and the 4 foll alt rows. 95(103) sts.
Patt until work measures 71(73)cm/28(28¾)in from beg, ending with a wrong side row.

Shape shoulders
Cast off 10(11) sts at beg of next 6 rows.
Cast off rem 35(37) sts.

LEFT FRONT
With 3¾mm (No 9/US 4) needles, cast on 59(63) sts.
Mst row: P1, [k1, p1] to end.
Mst a further 6 rows.
Inc row: Mst 17(18), m1, mst 25(27), m1, mst 17(18). 61(65) sts.
Change to 4mm (No 8/US 6) needles.
Work in patt thus:
1st row: Mst 9, [work 1st row of patt panel, mst 9] twice.
2nd row: Mst 9, [work 2nd row of patt panel, mst 9] twice.
These 2 rows set the position of the patt.
Cont in patt as set for a further 20 rows.
1st dec row: Mst 7, work 2tog, patt 17(19), work 2tog, mst 5, work 2tog, patt 17(19), work 2tog, mst 7. 57(61) sts. **
Patt another 11 rows.
*** 2nd dec row: Mst 6, work 2tog, patt 17(19), work 2tog, mst 3, work 2tog, patt 17(19), work 2tog, mst 6. 53(57) sts.
Patt a further 17 rows.
3rd dec row: Mst 5, work 2tog, patt 17(19), work 2tog, mst 1, work 2tog, patt 17(19), work 2tog, mst 5. 49(53) sts.

Patt a further 23 rows.

1st inc row: Mst 6, m1, patt 17(19), m1, mst 3, m1, patt 17(19), m1, mst 6. 53(57) sts.

Patt a further 17 rows.

2nd inc row: Mst 7, m1, patt 17(19), m1, mst 5, m1, patt 17(19), m1, mst 7. 57(61) sts.

Patt a further 11 rows.

3rd inc row: Mst 8, m1, patt 17(19), m1, mst 7, m1, patt 17(19), m1, mst 8. 61(65) sts.

Patt a further 15 rows – patt 16 rows here when working right front.

Shape armhole

Cast off 4 sts at beg of next row.

Patt 1 row – omit this row when working right front.

Dec 1 st at side edge on next row and the 4 foll alt rows. 52 (56) sts.

Patt a further 5 rows.

Shape neck ***

Next row: Patt to last 4 sts, turn and leave these sts on a safety-pin.

**** Dec 1 st at neck edge on the next row and the 9 foll 3rd rows. 38(42) sts.

Patt 1 row, then dec 1 st at neck edge on next row and the 7(8) foll alt rows. 30(33) sts.

Cont in patt until work measures the same as back to shoulder, ending at side edge.

Shape shoulder

Cast off 10(11) sts at beg of next and foll alt row. 10(11) sts.

Cast off rem 10(11) sts.

RIGHT FRONT

Work as left front to **.

Patt another 5 rows.

Buttonhole row: Mst 2, work 2tog, yrn, mst 2, patt to end.

Mark position for a further 6 buttons along left front, placing markers so that they are evenly spaced, having last marker 4 rows down from neck edge.

Working buttonholes to correspond with markers on left front, continue thus:

Patt a further 6 rows.

Work from left front from *** to ****.

Next row: Patt 4 and leave sts on a safety-pin, patt to end.

Work as left front from **** to end.

SLEEVES

With 3¾mm (No 9/US 4) needles, cast on 41(45) sts.

Work 9 rows in mst as given for back.

Inc row: Mst 8(9), m1, mst 25(27), m1, mst 8(9). 43(47) sts.

Change to 4mm (No 8/US 6) needles.

Work patt thus:

1st row (right side): Work 1st row of patt panel, mst 9, work 1st row of patt panel.

2nd row: Work 2nd row of patt panel, mst 9, work 2nd row of patt panel.

These 2 rows set the position of the patt.

Patt a further 4 rows.

Keeping continuity of patt, taking extra sts into mst as they occur, inc 1 st each end of next row and the 14(15) foll 8th rows. 73(79) sts.

Cont in patt until work measures 53cm/20¾in from beg, ending with a wrong side row.

Shape sleeve top

Dec 1 st each end of next row and the 3 foll alt rows. 65(71) sts.

Patt 1 row.

Cast off.

RIGHT HALF COLLAR

Join shoulder seams. With right side of right front facing, using 3¾mm (No 9/US 4) needles, sl the 4 sts from safety-pin on to needle, having point to inner edge, turn.

***** Next row: Inc, mst to end.

Mst 2 rows.

Keeping continuity of mst, inc 1 st at inside edge on next row and the 14 foll 3rd rows. 20 sts.

Cont in mst until collar fits up right front to shoulder, ending at outside edge.

Shape collar

Next row: Mst 12, turn, mst to end.

Mst 4 rows.

Rep last 6 rows, until inner edge of collar fits across from shoulder to centre back neck.

Cast off.

LEFT HALF COLLAR

With wrong side of left front facing, using 3¾mm (No 9 /US 4) needles, sl the sts from safety-pin on to needle, having point to inner edge, turn.

Work as right half collar from ***** to end.

TO MAKE UP

First, see basic information on page 7. Then set sleeves into armholes, sewing the last 8 row-ends of sleeve to cast-off sts at underarms. Join side and sleeve seams. Sew shaped edge of collar to neck edge. Join centre back seam. Sew on buttons.

Longline Aran Tunic

MATERIALS
28 x 50g balls of Jaeger Matchmaker Merino Aran.
Pair each of 3¾mm (No 9/US 4) and 4½mm (No 7/US 7) knitting needles.
A cable needle.

MEASUREMENTS

To fit bust size	86-97cm
	34-38in
Actual measurement	120cm
	47¼in
Length	72cm
	28in
Sleeve seam	44cm
	17¼in

TENSION
20 sts and 28 rows to 10cm/4in square, over patt, and panel A to measure 2.5cm/1in in width, panel B to measure 8cm/3in in width, panel C to measure 10cm/4in in width and panel D to measure 14cm/5½in in width on 4½mm (No 7/US 7) needles.

ABBREVIATIONS
C4 or 6B = Sl next 2 or 3 sts on to cable needle and leave at back, k2 or 3, then k2 or 3 from cable needle.
C4 or 6F = Sl next 2 or 3 sts on to cable needle and leave at front, k2 or 3, then k2 or 3 from cable needle.
T3B = Sl next st on to cable needle and leave at back, k2, then p1 from cable needle.
T3F = Sl next 2 sts on to cable needle and leave at front, p1, then k2 from cable needle.
T5R = Sl next 2 sts on to cable needle and leave at back, k3, then p2 from cable needle.
T5L = Sl next 3 sts on to cable needle and leave at front, p2, then k3 from cable needle.
T9F = Sl next 4 sts on to cable needle and leave at front, k4, p1, then k4 from cable needle.
C12R = Sl next 8 sts on to cable needle and leave at back, k4, sl last 4 sts from cable needle back on to left-hand needle and k these 4 sts, then k4 from cable needle.
C12L = Sl next 8 sts on to cable needle and leave at front, k4, sl last 4 sts from cable needle back on to left-hand needle and k these 4 sts, then k4 from cable needle.
m1 = Pick up loop lying between needles and p into back of it.
m1k = Pick up loop lying between needles and k into back of it.
See also page 7.

PATTERN PANEL A (worked over 10 sts)
1st row (right side): P2, k6, p2.
2nd row: K2, p6, k2.
3rd row: P2, k6, p2.
4th row: K2, p6, k2.
5th row: P2, C6F, p2.
6th row: K2, p6, k2.
These 6 rows form the patt for panel A.

PATTERN PANEL B (worked over 24 sts)
1st row (right side): K2, p2, k2, p4, k4, p4, k2, p2, k2.
2nd row: P2, k2, p2, k4, p4, k4, p2, k2, p2.
3rd row: K2, p2, k2, p4, C4B, p4, k2, p2, k2.
4th row: P2, k2, p2, k4, p4, k4, p2, k2, p2.
5th row: K2, p2, [T3F, p2, T3B] twice, p2, k2.
6th row: P2, k3, p2, [k2, p2] 3 times, k3, p2.
7th row: K2, p3, T3F, T3B, p2, T3F, T3B, p3, k2.
8th row: P2, k4, p4, k4, p4, k4, p2.
9th row: K2, p4, C4B, p4, C4B, p4, k2.
10th row: P2, k4, p4, k4, p4, k4, p2.
11th row: K2, p4, k4, p4, k4, p4, k2.
12th to 18th rows: Rep the 8th to 11th rows, once, then work the 8th to 10th rows again.
19th row: K2, p3, T3B, T3F, p2, T3B, T3F, p3, k2.
20th row: P2, k3, p2, [k2, p2] 3 times, k3, p2.
21st row: K2, p2, [T3B, p2, T3F] twice, p2, k2.
22nd to 24th rows: Work the 2nd to 4th rows, once.
25th to 28th rows: As 1st to 4th rows.
These 28 rows form the patt for panel B.

PATTERN PANEL C (worked over 34 sts)
1st row (right side): K2, p2, k6, [p4, k6] twice, p2, k2.
2nd row: P2, k2, p6, [k4, p6] twice, k2, p2.
3rd row: K2, p2, C6B, [p4, C6B] twice, p2, k2.
4th row: P2, k2, p6, [k4, p6] twice, k2, p2.
5th to 8th rows: As 1st to 4th rows.
9th row: K2, p2, k3, T5L, p2, k6, p2, T5R, k3, p2, k2.
10th row: P2, k2, [p3, k2] twice, p6, [k2, p3] twice, k2, p2.
11th row: K2, p2, T5L, T5L, k6, T5R, T5R, p2, k2.
12th row: P2, k4, p3, k2, p12, k2, p3, k4, p2.
13th row: K2, p4, T5L, C6F, C6F, T5R, p4, k2.
14th row: P2, k6, p18, k6, p2.
15th row: K2, p6, [C6B] 3 times, p6, k2.
16th row: P2, k6, p18, k6, p2.
17th row: K2, p4, T5R, C6F, C6F, T5L, p4, k2.
18th row: P2, k4, p3, k2, p12, k2, p3, k4, p2.
19th row: K2, p2, T5R, T5R, k6, T5L, T5L, p2, k2.
20th row: P2, k2, [p3, k2] twice, p6, [k2, p3] twice, k2, p2.
21st row: K2, p2, k3, T5R, p2, k6, p2, T5L, k3, p2, k2.
22nd to 28th rows: Work the 2nd to 8th rows, once.
These 28 rows form the patt for panel C.

PATTERN PANEL D (worked over 41 sts)
1st row (right side): K2, [p2, k4] 3 times, p1, [k4, p2] 3 times, k2.
2nd row: P2, [k2, p4] 3 times, k1, [p4, k2] 3 times, p2.

3rd row: K2, p2, k4, p2, C4F, p2, k4, p1, k4, p2, C4B, p2, k4, p2, k2.

4th row: P2, [k2, p4] 3 times, k1, [p4, k2] 3 times, p2.

5th and 6th rows: As 1st and 2nd rows.

7th row: K2, p2, k4, p2, C4F, p2, T9F, p2, C4B, p2, k4, p2, k2.

8th row: P2, [k2, p4] 3 times, k1, [p4, k2] 3 times, p2.

9th row: K2, p2, m1, [k4, p2] twice, k4, m1, p1, m1, [k4, p2] twice, k4, m1, p2, k2. 45 sts.

10th row: P2, k3, [p4, k2] twice, p4, k3, [p4, k2] twice, p4, k3, p2.

11th row: K2, p3, m1, k4, p2tog, C4F, p2tog, k4, m1, p3, m1, k4, p2tog, C4B, p2tog, k4, m1, p3, k2.

12th row: P2, k4, [p4, k1] twice, p4, k5, [p4, k1] twice, p4, k4, p2.

13th row: K2, p4, m1, k3, sl 1, k1, psso, k4, k2tog, k3, m1, p5, m1, k3, sl 1, k1, psso, k4, k2tog, k3, m1, p4, k2.

14th row: P2, k5, p12, k7, p12, k5, p2.

15th row: K2, p5, m1, k4, C4F, k4, m1, p7, m1, k4, C4B, k4, m1, p5, k2. 49 sts.

16th row: P2, k6, p12, k9, p12, k6, p2.

17th row: K2, p6, C12R, p9, C12L, p6, k2.

18th row: P2, k6, p12, k9, p12, k6, p2.

19th row: K2, p4, p2tog, k4, C4F, k4, p2tog, p5, p2tog, k4, C4B, k4, p2tog, p4, k2. 45 sts.

20th row: P2, k5, p12, k7, p12, k5, p2.

21st row: K2, p3, p2tog, [k4, m1] twice, k4, p2tog, p3, p2tog, [k4, m1] twice, k4, p2tog, p3, k2.

22nd row: P2, k4, [p4, k1] twice, p4, k5, [p4, k1] twice, p4, k4, p2.

23rd row: K2, p2, p2tog, k4, m1, p1, C4F, p1, m1, k4, p2tog, p1, p2tog, k4, m1, p1, C4B, p1, m1, k4, p2tog, p2, k2.

24th row: P2, k3, [p4, k2] twice, p4, k3, [p4, k2] twice, p4, k3, p2.

25th row: K2, p1, p2tog, [k4, p2] twice, k4, p3tog, [k4, p2] twice, k4, p2tog, p1, k2. 41 sts.

26th row: P2, [k2, p4] 3 times, k1, [p4, k2] 3 times, p2.

27th row: K2, p2, k4, p2, C4F, p2, T9F, p2, C4B, p2, k4, p2, k2.

28th row: P2, [k2, p4] 3 times, k1, [p4, k2] 3 times, p2.

These 28 rows form the patt for panel D.

BACK AND FRONT ALIKE

With 3¾mm (No 9/US 4) needles, cast on 172 sts.

1st rib row (right side): [K2, p2] twice, k4, [p2, k2] twice, p2, k4, [p2, k2] 11 times, p2, [k3, p2] 6 times, [k2, p2] 11 times, k4, [p2, k2] twice, p2, k4, [p2, k2] twice.

2nd rib row: [P2, k2] twice, p4, [k2, p2] twice, k2, p4, [k2, p2] 11 times, k2, [p3, k2] 6 times, [p2, k2] 11 times, p4, [k2, p2] twice, k2, p4, [k2, p2] twice.

Rep last 2 rows, 6 times more, then work the 1st row again.

Inc row: Rib 6, m1k, rib 2, m1k, rib 4, m1k, rib 2, m1k, rib 8, m1, rib 4, m1, rib 12, m1k, rib 2, m1k, rib 6, m1k, rib 2, m1k, rib 24, m1, [rib 5, m1] twice, rib 10, m1, rib 8, m1, rib 24, m1k, rib 2, m1k, rib 6, m1k, rib 2, m1k, rib 12, m1, rib 4, m1, rib 8, m1k, rib 2, m1k, rib 4, m1k, rib 2, m1k, rib 6. 197 sts.

Change to 4½mm (No 7/US 7) needles.

1st row: Work across 1st row of patt panels B, A, C, A, D, A, C, A and B.

2nd row: Work across 2nd row of patt panels B, A, C, A, D, A, C, A and B.

3rd row: Work across 3rd row of patt panels B, A, C, A, D, A, C, A and B.

4th row: Work across 4th row of patt panels B, A, C, A, D, A, C, A and B.

These 4 rows set position of the patt.

Cont in patt for a further 192 rows, marking the 136th of these rows for end of side seams.

Divide for neck

Next row: Patt 61, turn and leaving rem sts on a spare needle, work on these sts for first half of neck.

First half neck

Dec 1 st at neck edge on next 13 rows. 48 sts.

Patt 1 row here when working second half of neck.

Shape shoulder

Cast off 16 sts at beg of the next row and the foll alt row.

Patt 1 row.

Cast off rem 16 sts.

Second half neck

With right side facing, sl the centre 79 sts on to a st holder, rejoin yarn to inner edge of rem 61 sts and patt to end.

Work as first half of neck, noting variation.

SLEEVES

With 3¾mm (No 9/US 4) needles, cast on 56 sts.

1st rib row: [P2, k2] 3 times, p2, [k3, p2] 6 times, [k2, p2] 3 times.

2nd rib row: [K2, p2] 3 times, k2, [p3, k2] 6 times, [p2, k2] 3 times.

Rep last 2 rows, 6 times more, then work the 1st row again.

Inc row: Rib 14, m1, rib 8, m1, rib 10, [m1, rib 5] twice, m1, rib 14. 61 sts.

Change to 4½mm (No 7/US 7) needles.

1st row (right side): Work across 1st row of patt panels A, D, A.

2nd row: Work across 2nd row of patt panels A, D, A.

3rd row: Work across 3rd row of patt panels A, D, A.

4th row: Work across the 4th row of patt panels A, D, A.

These 4 rows set position of the patt for the sleeves.

Keeping continuity of patt as set, taking extra sts into k2, p2 rib as they occur, inc 1 st each end of the next row and the 24 foll 4th rows. 111 sts.

Cont in patt for a further 11 rows.

Cast off.

NECKBAND

Join right shoulder seam. With right side facing, using 3¾mm (No 9/US 4) needles, pick up and k16 sts down first half neck, * work across centre sts thus:

K2tog, k1, p2, k2, p2, k3tog, sl 1, k2tog, psso, p2, k2, p2tog, p1, [k2tog] twice, p2, k2tog, sl 1, k1, psso, p2, [k2tog] twice, p1,

p2tog, [k2tog] twice, p2, [k2tog] twice, p2, [k2tog] twice, p2tog, p1, k2, p2, k3tog, sl 1, k2tog, psso, p2, k2, p2, k1, k2tog *, pick up and k15 sts up second half neck, 15 sts down first half neck, work from * to * once, pick up and k16 sts up second half neck. 170 sts.

1st rib row: P2, [k2, p2] to end.

2nd rib row: K2, [p2, k2] to end.

Rep last 2 rows, 7 times more, then work the 1st row again.

Cast off in rib.

TO MAKE UP

Join left shoulder seam and neckband.

Sew cast-off edge of sleeves to row-ends above markers on back and front. Join side and sleeve seams.

Argyle Twinset

MATERIALS

Cardigan: 4 x 50g balls of Rowan True 4 ply Botany in Aqua (M).
1 ball of the same yarn in each of Cream, Green and Lilac.
6(7:8) buttons.

Jumper: 4 x 50g balls of Rowan True 4 ply Botany in Aqua (M).
1 ball of the same yarn in each of Cream, Green and Lilac.
3 buttons.

For either garment: A pair each of 2¾mm (No 12/US 2) and
3¼mm (No 10/US 3) knitting needles.

MEASUREMENTS

To fit ages	6-12 months	12-18 months	2-3 years
Cardigan			
Actual chest measurement	59	64.5	70.5cm
	23½	25¼	27¾in
Length	28	33	39cm
	11	13	15¼in
Sleeve seam	24	24.5	27cm
	9½	10	10½in
Jumper			
Actual chest measurement	55	60.5	68cm
	21¾	23¾	26¾in
Length	28	33	39cm
	11	13	15¼in
Sleeve seam	6	7	8cm
	2½	2¾	3in

TENSION

28 sts and 36 rows to 10cm/4in square over st st on 3¼mm
(No 10/US 3) needles.

ABBREVIATIONS

See page 7.

NOTE

Read chart from right to left on right side (K) rows and from left to
right on wrong side (P) rows. When working pattern, strand yarn
not in use loosely across back of work to keep fabric elastic.

CARDIGAN

BACK AND FRONTS (worked in one piece to armholes)
With 2¾mm (No 12/US 2) needles and M, cast on 173
(189:205) sts.

1st row (right side): K2, [p1, k1] to last 3 sts, p1, k2.
2nd row: K1, [p1, k1] to end.
Rep last 2 rows, once.
Buttonhole row: Rib 3, yrn, p2tog, rib to end.
Cont in rib until work measures 3cm/1¼in from beg, ending with
the 2nd row.
Next row: Rib 6 and leave these sts on a safety-pin for buttonhole

band, change to 3¼mm (No 10/US 3) needles and k to last 6 sts,
turn and leave these 6 sts on a safety-pin for button band.
161(177:193) sts.
Beg with a p row, work 3(5:7) rows in st st.
Beg with a k row, work the 15 rows of chart.
Beg with a p row, cont in M only, work in st st until work measures
16(19:23)cm/6¼(7½:9)in from beg, ending with a k row.

Divide for back and fronts

Next row: P40(44:48) and leave these sts on a spare needle for
left front, p81(89:97) and leave these sts on a spare needle for
back, p40(44:48) and work on these sts for right front.

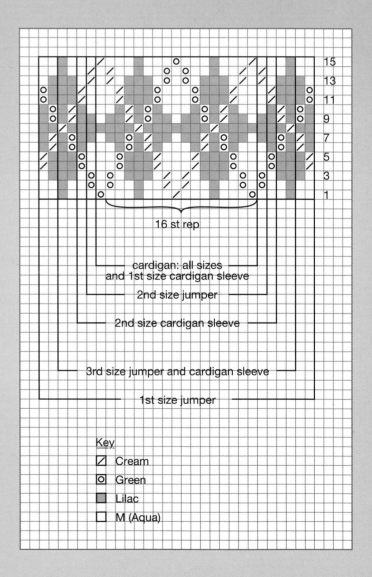

15
13
11
9
7
5
3
1

16 st rep

cardigan: all sizes
and 1st size cardigan sleeve

2nd size jumper

2nd size cardigan sleeve

3rd size jumper and cardigan sleeve

1st size jumper

Key

⧄ Cream
⊙ Green
▨ Lilac
☐ M (Aqua)

Right front
Shape armhole
Work 1 row.
Cast off 2 sts at beg of next row and the 1(2:2) foll alt rows.
Work 1 row, then cast off 2(1:2) sts at beg of next row.
** Cont in st st until work measures 23.5(28:33)cm/9¼(11:13)in from beg, ending at front edge.
Shape neck
Next row: Work 5(6:7) sts and leave these sts on a safety-pin, work to end.
Dec 1 st at neck edge on the next 11 rows. 18(20:22) sts.
Cont in st st until work measures 28(33:39)cm/11(13:15¼)in from beg, ending at armhole edge.
Shape shoulder
Cast off 9(10:11) sts at beg of next row.
Work 1 row.
Cast off rem 9(10:11) sts.

Back
Shape armholes
With right side of work facing, rejoin M to 81(89:97) sts left for back.
Cast off 2 sts at beg of next 4(6:6) rows, then cast off 2(1:2) sts at beg of next 2 rows. 69(75:81) sts.
Cont in st st until work measures 28(33:39)cm/11(13:15¼)in from beg, ending with a wrong side row.
Shape shoulders
Cast off 9(10:11) sts at beg of next 4 rows.
Leave rem 33(35:37) sts on a st holder.

Left front
Shape armhole
With right side facing, rejoin M to inner edge of 40(44:48) sts of left front.
Cast off 2 sts at beg of next row and the 1 (2:2) foll alt rows.
Work 1 row, then cast off 2(1:2) sts at beg of next row. 34(37:40) sts.
Work as right front from ** to end.

SLEEVES
With 2¾mm (No 12/US 2) needles and M, cast on 46(50:54) sts.
1st row: [k1, p1] to end.
Rep this row until work measures 3.5(4:4.5)cm/1¼(1½:1¾)in from beg, ending with an even-numbered row, inc 1 st in centre of last row. 47(51:55) sts.
Change to 3¼mm (No 10/US 3) needles.
Beg with a k row, work 4 rows in st st, inc 1 st each end of the 3rd of these rows. 49(53:57) sts.
Beg with a k row, work the 15 rows of chart and taking extra sts into patt as they occur, inc 1 st each end of the 3rd, 7th, 11th and 15th of these rows. 57(61:65) sts.
Cont with M only and beg with a p row, work 3 rows in st st.
Cont in st st, inc 1 st each end of next row and the 7(8:9) foll 4th rows. 73(79:85) sts.
Cont in st st until work measures 24(25.5:27)cm/9½(10:10½)in from beg, ending with a p row.

Shape top
Cast off 2 sts at beg of next 4(6:6) rows, then cast off 2(1:2) sts at beg of next 2 rows. 61(65:69) sts.
Cast off.

BUTTON BAND
With right side facing, using 2¾mm (No 12/US 2) needles, rejoin M to inner edge of 6 sts on left front safety-pin and inc, rib to end. 7 sts.
Work in rib until band is long enough when slightly stretched to fit up front to neck edge, ending at inside edge.
Leave sts on a safety-pin.

BUTTONHOLE BAND
First, on button band, mark position of 1st button to correspond with first buttonhole worked at beg of back and front, then mark positions for a further 4(5:6) buttons, having them evenly spaced to allow for a further buttonhole to be worked in neckband. With wrong side facing, using 2¾mm (No 12/US 2) needles, rejoin M to inner edge of 6 sts on right front safety-pin and inc, rib to end. 7 sts.
Work to match button band, working buttonholes as before to correspond with marked positions.

NECKBAND
Join shoulder seams. With right side facing, using 2¾mm (No 12/US 2) needles and M, sl the 7 buttonhole band sts on to needle, k5(6:7) from right front neck, then pick up and k14 sts up right front neck, k the 33(35:37) at back neck, pick up and k14 sts down left front neck, k5(6:7) from left front neck, rib 7 button band sts. 85(89:93) sts.
Work in rib for 6 rows, working a buttonhole as before at the beg of the 4th of these rows.
Cast off in rib.

TO MAKE UP
Set in sleeves. Join side and sleeve seams. Sew on front bands. Sew on buttons.

JUMPER
BACK
With 2¾mm (No 12/US 2) needles and M, cast on 77(85:91) sts.
1st row (right side): K1, [p1, k1] to end.
2nd row: P1, [k1, p1] to end.
Rep last 2 rows for 3cm/1¼in, ending with an even-numbered row.
Change to 3¼mm (No 10/US 3) needles.
Beg with a k row, work in st st until work measures 16(19:23)cm/6¼(7½:9)in from beg, ending with a p row.
Shape armholes
Cast off 2 sts at beg of next 6(8:8) rows, then 2(1:1) sts at beg of next 2 rows. 61(67:73) sts.
Work 2 rows in st st.
Beg with a k row, work the 15 rows of chart.
Cont with M only, work 1(3:5) rows in st st. ***
Divide for back opening

Next row: K28(31:34) sts, turn and leaving rem sts on a spare needle, work on these sts for right half back.

Right half back
Cont in st st until work measures 28(33:39)cm/11(13:15½)in from beg, ending at side edge.

Shape shoulder
Cast off 9(10:11) sts at beg of next row and the foll alt row.
Work 1 row – omit this row when working left half back.
Leave rem 10(11:12) sts on a st holder.

Left half back
With right side facing, sl centre 5 sts on to a safety-pin, rejoin M to inner edge of rem 28(31:34) sts and k to end.
Work as right half back, noting variation.

FRONT
Work as back to *** .
Work 2 rows.

Divide for neck
Next row: K22(24:26) sts, turn and leaving rem sts on a spare needle, work on these sts for left front neck.

Left front neck
Dec 1 st at neck edge on the next and the 3 foll alt rows. 18(20:22) sts.
Cont until work measures 28(33:39)cm/11(13:15¼)in from beg, ending at side edge.

Shape shoulder
Cast off 9(10:11) sts at beg of next row.
Work 1 row.
Cast off rem 9(10:11) sts.

Right front neck
With right side facing, sl centre 17(19:21) sts on to a st holder, rejoin M to inner edge of rem 22(24:26) sts and k to end.
Work as left front neck.

SLEEVES
With 2¾mm (No 12/US 2) needles and M, cast on 60(62:64) sts.
1st row (right side): [K1, p1] to end.
Rep this row 3 times more.
Change to 3¼mm (No 10/US 3) needles.
Beg with a k row, work 2 rows in st st.
Cont in st st, inc 1 st each end of next row and the 5(6:7) foll 3rd rows. 72(76:80) sts.
Cont in st st until work measures 6(7:8)cm/2¼(2¾:3)in from beg, ending with a p row.

Shape top
Cast off 2(2:1) st(s) at beg of next 6(2:2) rows, then 1st at beg of next 2(8:8) rows. 58(64:70) sts.
Work 1 row.
Cast off.

BUTTON BAND
With 2¾mm (No 12/US 2) needles and M, cast on 7 sts.
1st row (right side): P1, [k1, p1] twice, k2.

2nd row: K1, [p1, k1] to end.
Rep last 2 rows until work fits up row-ends of back opening to neck edge, ending with a wrong side row.
Leave sts on a safety-pin.

BUTTONHOLE BAND
First mark positions for 2 buttons on button band having them evenly spaced to allow for 3rd buttonhole to be worked in neckband.
With right side facing, using 2¾mm (No 12/US 2) needles, rejoin M to 5 sts at centre back opening and k3, m1, k2, turn, cast on 1 st. 7 sts.
1st row (wrong side): K1, [p1, k1] to end.
2nd row: K2, p1, [k1, p1] twice.
Working buttonholes to match marked positions on button band thus:
Rib 3, yrn, p2tog, rib 2, work to match button band.

NECKBAND
Join shoulder seams. With right side facing, using 2¾mm (No 12/US 2) needles and M, rib the 7 sts of buttonhole band, k the 10(11:12) sts of left half back, pick up and k17 (17:19) sts down left front neck, k the 17(19:21) sts at centre front, dec 0(0:2) pick up and k17(17:19) sts up right front neck, k the 10(11:12) sts of right half back, then rib the 7 sts of button band. 85(89:95) sts.
Work in rib for 6 rows, making a buttonhole as before at the beg of the 4th of these rows.
Cast off in rib.

TO MAKE UP
Set in sleeves. Join side and sleeve seams. Sew on button and buttonhole bands, catching cast-on edge of button band behind buttonhole band. Sew on buttons.

Shawl Collared Sweater

MATERIALS
11 (11:12) 100g balls of Rowan Super Chunky Tweed.
Pair each of 8mm (No 0/US 11) and 9mm (No 00/US 13) knitting needles.

MEASUREMENTS

To fit sizes	small	medium	large
Actual chest measurement	124	132	140cm
	48¾	52	55in
Length	68	69	70cm
	26¾	27	27½in
Sleeve seam with	46	47	48cm
cuff turned back	18	18½	19in

TENSION
10 sts and 16 rows to 10cm/4in square over st st on 9mm (No 00/US 13) needles.

ABBREVIATIONS
See page 7.

BACK
With 8mm (No 0/US 11) needles, cast on 62(66:70) sts.
1st row: K2 [p2, k2] to end.
2nd row: P2, [k2, p2] to end.
Rep last 2 rows for 6cm/2¼in.
Change to 9mm (No 00/US 13) needles.
Beg with a k row, work in st st until back measures 43cm/17in from beg, ending with a p row.
Mark each end of last row for side seams**.
Cont in st st for a further 25(26:27)cm/9¾(10¼:10½)in, ending with a p row.
Shape shoulders
Cast off 10(11:12) sts at beg of next 4 rows.
Cast off rem 22 sts.

FRONT
Work as back to **.
Cont in st st for a further 5(6:7)cm/2(2¼:2¾)in, ending with a wrong side row.
Divide for neck
Next row: K31(33:35), turn and leaving rem sts on a spare needle, work on these sts for left front neck.
Left front neck
Next row: P to end.
Next row: K to last 4 sts, k2tog, k2.
Rep last 2 rows, 10 times more. 20(22:24) sts.
Cont in st st until front measures same as back to shoulder shaping, ending at side edge.

Shape shoulder
Cast off 10(11:12) sts at beg of next row.
Work 1 row.
Cast off rem 10(11:12) sts.
Right front neck: With right side facing, rejoin yarn to inner edge of sts on spare needle and k to end.
Next row: P to end.
Next row: K2, sl 1, k1, psso, k to end.
Complete as given for left front neck.

SLEEVES
With 9mm (No 00/US13) needles, cast on 26(26:30) sts.
Work 8cm/3¼in in rib as given for back.
Change to 8mm (No 0/US 11) needles and work in rib for a further 7cm/2¾in, ending with a right side row.
Inc row: Rib2, inc, [rib 3 (2:4), inc] to last 3(2:2) sts, rib to end.
32(34:36) sts.
Change to 9mm (No 00/US 13) needles.
Beg with a k row, st st 2 rows.
Keeping continuity of st st, inc 1 st each end of the next row and the 8 foll 6th rows. 50(52:54) sts.
Cont in st st until sleeve measures 54(55:56) cm/ 21¼(21½:22)in from beg, ending with a p row.
Cast off.

SHAWL COLLAR
With 8mm (No 0/US 11) needles, cast on 22 sts.
1st row: K2, [p2, k2] to end.
2nd row: Cast on 4 sts, p2, k2 across these 4 sts, rib to end.
3rd row: Cast on 4 sts, k2, p2 across these 4 sts, rib to end.
Rep the 3rd and 4th rows, 6 times more. 78 sts.
Work in rib for a further 3cm/1¼ in.
With 9mm (No 00/US 13) needles, cast off loosely in rib.

TO MAKE UP
Join shoulder seams. Beg and ending at centre front, sew cast-on edge of collar to neck edge. Overlap left side over right and catch short row-ends at left side to right front and row-ends at right side behind left side. Sew cast-off edge of sleeves to row-ends above markers on back and front. Join side and sleeve seams.

Beret

MATERIALS

1 x 50g ball of Jaeger Baby Merino 4 ply in Stone (M).
A ball of the same yarn in each of Navy (A), Cream, Light Blue and Yellow.
1 x 50g ball of Jaeger Matchmaker Merino 4 ply in each of Red and Mid Blue.
A set of four 2¾mm (No 12/US 2) and 3¼mm (No 10/US 3) double pointed knitting needles.

MEASUREMENTS

To fit ages   6–12 months (2–4:4–6:8–10) years

TENSION

32 sts and 32 rows to 10cm/4in square over patt on 3¼mm (No 10/US 3) needles.

ABBREVIATIONS

See page 7.

NOTE

When working in rounds, work (K) on every round and read chart from right to left on every round. When working pattern, strand yarn not in use loosely across back of work to keep fabric elastic.

TO MAKE

With set of four 2¾mm (No 12/US 2) double pointed needles and M, cast on 92(102:112:122) sts.
Arrange sts on to 3 needles and with 4th needle, cont thus:
Work 4 rounds in k1, p1 rib.
Inc round: * Rib 1(2:3:4), [inc, inc, inc, rib 1] 11(12:13:14) times, inc; rep from * once more. 160(176:192:208) sts.
Change to set of four 3¼mm (No 10/US 3) needles.
Reading every row of chart from right to left, working in rounds and in st st, every round k, work 10 rounds in patt from Chart 1.
With M, work 2(3:5:5) rounds, dec 4 sts evenly across the last of these rounds on the 1st and 4th sizes only and inc 4 sts evenly on the 2nd size only. 156(180:192:204) sts.
Work 15 rounds in patt from Chart 2.
With M, work 1(2:3:4) round(s).
1st dec round: [K4, k2tog] to end. 130(150:160:170) sts.
Work 13 rounds from Chart 3.
2nd dec round: * [K1M, 1A] twice, with M, k3tog, k1A, 1M, 1A; rep from * to end. 104 (120:128:136) sts.
3rd dec round: [K1A, 1M, 1A, with M, k3tog, k1A, 1M] to end. 78(90:96:102) sts.
Cont with M only.
4th dec round: [K2, k3tog, k1] to end. 52(60:62:64:68) sts.
5th dec round: [K1, k3tog] to end. 26(30:32:34) sts.
6th dec round: [K2tog] to end. 13(15:16:17) sts.
Break off yarn leaving a long end, thread end through rem sts, draw up tightly and secure.

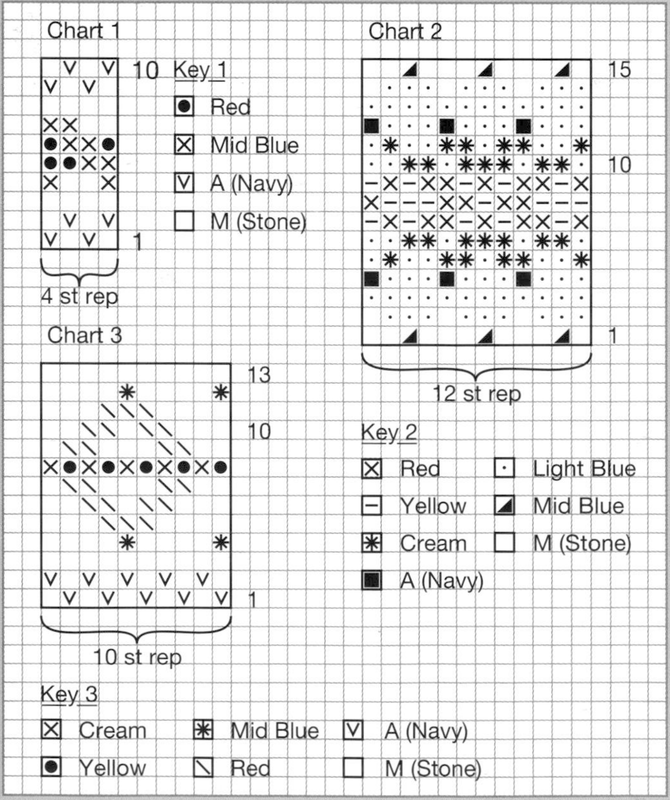

Chart 1

10

1

4 st rep

Key 1

- ● Red
- ☒ Mid Blue
- ☑ A (Navy)
- ☐ M (Stone)

Chart 2

15

10

1

12 st rep

Chart 3

13

10

1

10 st rep

Key 2

- ☒ Red
- ⊟ Yellow
- ✳ Cream
- ■ A (Navy)
- · Light Blue
- ◢ Mid Blue
- ☐ M (Stone)

Key 3

- ☒ Cream
- ● Yellow
- ✳ Mid Blue
- ╲ Red
- ☑ A (Navy)
- ☐ M (Stone)

Fair Isle Sweater with Socks

MATERIALS

Sweater: 3 x 50g balls of Jaeger Baby Merino 4 ply in Stone (M).
1 x 50g ball of the same yarn in each of Cream, Light Blue, Navy and Yellow.
1 x 50g ball of Jaeger Matchmaker Merino 4 ply in each of Red and Mid Blue.
Pair each of 2¾mm (No 12/US 2) and 3¼mm (No 10/US 3) knitting needles.
Set of four 2¾mm (No 12/US 2) double pointed knitting needles.
Socks: 1 x 50g ball of Jaeger Baby Merino 4 ply in Stone (M).
Small amounts of the same yarn in each of Cream, Navy and Yellow.
Small amounts of Jaeger Matchmaker Merino 4 ply in each of Red and Mid Blue.
Pair each of 2¾mm (No 12/US 2) and 3¼mm (No 10/US 3) knitting needles.
A set of four 3¼mm (No 10/US 3) double pointed knitting needles.

MEASUREMENTS

To fit ages	9	12	18 months
Actual chest measurement	60	64	70cm
	23½	25¼	27½in
Length	32	36	39cm
	12½	14¼	15½in
Sleeve seam	18	21	24cm
	7	8¼	9½in
Scoks to fit foot size	13cm		
	5in		

TENSION

32 sts and 32 rows to 10cm/4in square over patt on 3¼mm (No10/US 3) needles.

ABBREVIATIONS

See page 7.

NOTE

Read chart from right to left on right side (K) rows and from left to right on wrong side (P) rows. When working pattern, strand yarn not in use loosely across back of work to keep fabric elastic.

SWEATER
BACK

With 2¾mm (No 12/US 2) needles and M, cast on 81(85:93) sts.
lst rib row (right side): K1, [p1, k1] to end.
2nd rib row: P1, [k1, p1] to end.
Rep lst 2 rows until work measures 3cm/1in from beg, ending with a right side row.
Inc row: Rib 1(4:3), [inc, rib 4(3:3), inc, rib 4] to end. 97(103:113) sts.
Change to 3¼mm (No 10/US 3) needles.

Beg with a k row, work in st st and patt from chart until work measures 19(22:24)cm/7½(8½:9½)in from beg, ending with a wrong side row.
Mark each end of last row for end of side seams.
Cont in patt until work measures 32(36:39)cm/12½(14:15½)in from beg, ending with a wrong side row.

Shape shoulders

Cast off 15(16:18) sts at beg of next 4 rows.
Leave rem 37(39:41) sts on a st holder.

POCKET LININGS (make 2)

With 3¼mm (No 10/US 3) needles and M, cast on 26 sts.
Beg with a k row, work in st st until work measures 6.5cm/2½in from beg, ending with a wrong side row.
Leave these sts on a st holder.

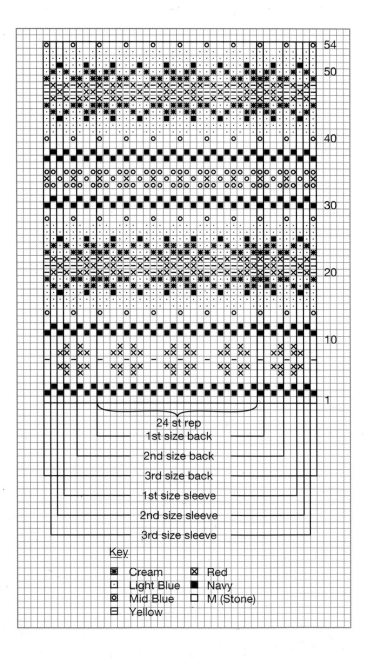

	54	
	50	
	40	
	30	
	20	
	10	
	1	

24 st rep
1st size back
2nd size back
3rd size back
1st size sleeve
2nd size sleeve
3rd size sleeve

Key

✴ Cream	⊠ Red
⊡ Light Blue	■ Navy
⊚ Mid Blue	☐ M (Stone)
⊟ Yellow	

FRONT

Work as back until front measures 11cm/4¼in from beg, ending with a wrong side row.

Next pocket row: Patt 9(10:11), * sl next 26 sts on to a st holder, patt across the 26 sts of one pocket lining *, patt 27(31:39), work from * to * once, patt 9(10:11) sts. 97(103:113) sts.

Cont in patt until work measures 19(22:24)cm/7½(8½:9½)in from beg, ending with a wrong side row.

Mark each end of last row for end of side seams.

Cont in patt until work measures 27(31:34)cm/10½(12¼:13¼)in from beg, ending with a wrong side row.

Shape neck

Next row: Patt 39(41:45) sts, turn and leaving rem sts on a spare needle, work on these sts for left front neck.

Left front neck

Dec 1 st at neck edge on next 9 rows. 30(32:36) sts.

Cont in patt until work measures same as back to shoulder, ending at side edge.

Shape shoulder

Cast off 15(16:18) sts at beg of next row.

Patt 1 row.

Cast off rem 15(16:18) sts.

Right front neck

With right side facing, sl centre 19(21:23) sts on to a st holder, rejoin yarns to inner edge of rem 39(41:45) sts and work as left front neck.

SLEEVES

With 2¾mm (No 12/US 2) needles and M, cast on 49(51:53) sts.
Work 3cm/1in in rib as given for back.

Inc row: Rib 6(3:3), inc, [rib 3(4:4), inc] to last 6(2:4) sts, rib to
end. 59 (61:63) sts.

Change to 3¼mm (No 10/US 3) needles.
Beg with a k row, work 2 rows in st st and patt from chart.
Keeping continuity of patt to match chart, inc 1 st each end of the
next row and the 11(13:15) foll 3rd rows. 83(89:95) sts.
Cont in patt until work measures 18(21:24)cm/7(8¼:9½)in from
beg, ending with a wrong side row.
Cast off.

COLLAR

Join shoulder seams. With right side facing, sl first 9(10:11) sts
from centre front on to a safety-pin. Using three of the set of four
2¾mm (No 12/US 2) needles, rejoin M and k rem 10(11:12) sts
from centre front, pick up and k18 sts up right front neck, k the
37(39:41) sts at back neck, inc 4 sts evenly across these sts, pick
up and k18 sts down left front neck, then k the 9(11:10) sts from
safety-pin. 96(100:104) sts.

Using 4th needle, work in k1, p1 rib in rounds for 1.5cm/½in, inc 1
st at end of last round, turn. 97(101:105) sts.
Working backwards and forwards in rows, work in rib until collar
measures 4cm/1½in.
Change to 3¼mm (No 10/US 3) double pointed needles and work
in rib until collar measures 6(7:8)cm/2¼(2¾:3¼)in.
Cast off loosely in rib.

POCKET TOPS

With right side facing, using 2¾mm (No 12/US 2) needles and M,
k across the 26 sts on st holder of one pocket top, inc 1 st at
centre of row. 27 sts.
Beg with the 2nd row, work 7 rows in rib as given for back.
Cast off in rib.

TO MAKE UP

Sew cast-off edge of sleeves to row-ends above markers on back
and front. Join side and sleeve seams. Catch pocket linings to
wrong side and row-ends of pocket tops to right side.

SOCKS (make 2)

With 2¾mm (No 12/US 2) needles and M, cast on 49 sts for cuff.
Work 4 rows in rib as given for back of sweater.
Change to 3¼mm (No 10/US 3) needles.
Beg with a k row, work the 13th to 29th rows of chart as given for
1st size back of sweater, dec 6 sts evenly across the last of these
rows. 43 sts.
Change to 2¾mm (No 12/US 2) needles.
Cont with M only, and beg with the 1st right side row (thus
reversing the fabric), work 12cm/4¾in in rib as given for back,
ending with a wrong side row.
Change to 3¼mm (No 10/US 3) needles.
Beg with a k row, work 4 rows in st st.
Break off yarn.
With set of four 3¼mm (No 10/US 3) double pointed needles,
divide sts on to 3 needles as follows:
Sl first 9 sts on to first needle, next 12 sts on to second needle
and foll 12 sts on to 3rd needle, sl last 10 sts on to other end of
first needle.
Using 4th needle cont thus:

Shape heel

With right side facing, rejoin M to the 19 sts on first needle, k9,
k2tog, k8, turn.
Work on these 18 sts only.
Beg with a p row, work 9 rows in st st.
Next row: K13, k2tog tbl, turn.
Next row: Sl 1, p7, p2tog, turn.
Next row: Sl 1, k7, k2tog tbl, turn.
Next row: Sl 1, p7, p2tog, turn.

Rep last 2 rows, twice more. 10 sts.
Break off yarn.
Re-arrange sts on 3 needles thus:
Sl first 5 sts of heel on to safety-pin, place marker here to indicate
beg of round. Rejoin M to rem sts. With first needle k5, then pick
up and k8 sts along side of heel, k5, with second needle k14,
with third needle k5, then pick up and k8 sts along other side of
heel, finally k5 from safety-pin. 50 sts.
K1 round.
Using 4th needle cont thus:
Next round: K12, k2tog, k to last 14 sts, k2tog tbl, k12.
K1 round.
Next round: K11, k2tog, k to last 13 sts, k2tog tbl, k11.
K1 round.
Cont in this way, dec 1 st each side of heel on the next and 2 foll
alt rounds. 40 sts.
Cont without further shaping until work measures 11cm/4¼in from
back of heel.

Shape toe

Next round: [K7, k2tog, k2, k2tog tbl, k7] twice.
K1 round.
Next round: [K6, k2tog, k2, k2tog tbl, k6] twice.
K1 round.
Cont in this way, dec 4 sts on the next and 2 foll alt rounds. 20
sts.
Divide sts on to two needles for sole and instep and graft sts tog.
Join back seam, reversing seam for cuff edge to allow for fold
back. Fold back cuff.

Fair Isle Baby Wrap

MATERIALS

3 x 50g balls of Jaeger Merino 4 ply in Stone (M).
1 ball of the same yarn in each of Navy, Light Blue, Cream, Pink and Lemon.
1 ball of Jaeger Matchmaker 4 ply in each of Maroon and Red.
Pair each of 3¼mm (No 10/US 3) and 2¾ mm (No 12/US 2) knitting needles. A medium size crochet hook.

MEASUREMENTS

Approximately 47.5 x 74cm/18¾ x 29in.

TENSION

36 sts and 32 rows to 10cm/4in square over st st on 3¼mm (No 10/US 3) needles.

ABBREVIATIONS

Dc, double crochet; tr, treble; ss, slip st.
Also see page 7.

NOTE

Read chart from right to left on right side (K) rows and from left to right on wrong side (P) rows. When working pattern, strand yarn not in use loosely across back of work to keep fabric elastic.

TO MAKE

With 2¾mm (No 12/US 2) needles and M, cast on 167 sts.
K4 rows.
Change to 3¼mm (No 10/US 3) needles.
Using small ball of M at each side and twisting yarns together on wrong side at joins, work in patt as follows:
1st row (right side): K3M, work 1st row of chart to last 3 sts, k3M.
2nd row: K3M, work 2nd row of chart to last 3 sts, k3M.
3rd to 20th rows: Keeping 3 sts at each end in gst and in M, work

the 3rd to 20th rows of chart.
These 20 rows form a rep of the patt.
Rep the last 20 rows, 10 times more.
Work the 1st to 7th rows again.
Change to 2¾ mm (No 12/US 2) needles.
K4 rows with M.
Cast off.

CROCHET EDGING

With right side facing, using medium size crochet hook and M, beg at corner of one short edge, [work 3dc in corner, 96dc along short edge, 3dc in corner, 162dc along side edge] twice, then ss in first dc. 528dc.
Next row: Ss in next dc, [3tr in same dc as ss, * miss 2dc, ss in next dc, 2tr in same dc as ss*; work from * to * 31 times more, miss 2dc, ss in next dc, 3tr in same dc as ss, work from * to * 54 times, miss 2dc, ss in next dc] twice, miss next dc, ss in 1st tr at beg.
Fasten off.

Key

Symbol	Colour
◫	Red
⊟	Lemon
⊠	Pink
⊡	Maroon
◪	Cream
⊙	Light Blue
⬤	Navy
☐	M (Stone)

20

10

1

edge st   8 st rep

Chenille Jacket

MATERIALS

7(8:9) 100g balls of Rowan Chunky Cotton Chenille.
Pair each of 4mm (No 8/US 6) and 4½mm (No 7/US 7) knitting needles.
6 buttons.

MEASUREMENTS

To fit bust sizes	86	91	97cm
	34	36	38in
Actual measurement	102	107	112cm
	40	42	44in
Length	72	73	74cm
	28¼	28¾	29in
Sleeve seam	46	46	46cm
	18	18	18in

TENSION

16 sts and 24 rows to 10cm/4 in square over st st on 4½mm (No 7/US 7) needles.

ABBREVIATIONS

See page 7.

RIGHT HALF BACK

With 4mm (No 8/US 6) needles, cast on 48(50:52) sts.
1st mst row (right side): [K1, p1] to end.
2nd mst row: [P1, k1] to end.
Rep last 2 rows, twice more.
Change to 4½mm (No 7/US 7) needles.
1st row: K to last 4 sts, mst 4.
2nd row: Mst 4, p to end.
3rd to 22nd rows: Rep the last 2 rows, 10 times more.
23rd row: K3, sl 1, k1, psso, k25(26:27), k2tog, k12(13:14), mst 4. 46 (48:50) sts.
24th row: Mst 4, p to end.
25th row: K to last 4 sts, mst 4.
26th to 30th rows: Rep 24th and 25th rows, twice more, then work the 24th row again.
31st dec row: K3, sl 1, k1, psso, k23(24:25), k2tog, k12(13:14), mst 4. 44 (46:48) sts.
32nd to 38th rows: Work 7 rows as set.
39th dec row: K3, sl 1, k1, psso, k21(22:23), k2tog, k12(13:14), mst 4. 42 (44:46) sts.
40th to 46th row: Work 7 rows as set.
47th dec row: K3, sl 1, k1, psso, k19(20:21), k2tog, k12(13:14), mst 4. 40 (42:44) sts. **
48th row: Work 1 row as set.
49th row: K to last 4 sts, cast off 4.
Break yarn and leave rem 36(38:40) sts on a spare needle.

LEFT HALF BACK

With 4mm (No 8/US 6) needles, cast on 48(50:52) sts.
1st mst row (right side): [K1, p1] to end.
2nd mst row: [P1, k1] to end.
Rep last 2 rows, twice more.
Change to 4½mm (No 7/US 7) needles.
1st row: Mst 4, k to end.
2nd row: P to last 4 sts, mst 4.
3rd to 22nd rows: Rep the last 2 rows, 10 times more.
23rd dec row: Mst 4, k12(13:14), sl 1, k1, psso, k25(26:27), k2tog, k3. 46(48:50) sts.
24th row: P to last 4 sts, mst 4.
25th row: Mst 4, k to end.
26th to 30th rows: Rep the 24th and 25th rows, twice more, then work the 24th row again.
31st dec row: Mst 4, k12(13:14), sl 1, k1, psso, k23(24:25), k2tog, k3. 44(46:48) sts.
32nd row to 38th rows: Work 7 rows as set.
39th dec row: Mst 4, k12(13:14), sl 1, k1, psso, k21(22:23), k2tog, k3. 42(44:46) sts.
40th to 46th rows: Work 7 rows as set.
47th row: Mst 4, k12(13:14), sl 1, k1, psso, k19(20:21), k2tog, k3. 40(42:44) sts. ***
48th and 49th rows: Work 2 rows as set.
50th joining row: P40(42:44) sts of left half back, then p across the 36(38:40) sts of right half back. 76(80:84) sts.
51st to 54th rows: Beg with a k row, work 4 rows in st st.
55th dec row: K3, sl 1, k1, psso, k17(18:19), k2tog, k28(30:32), sl 1, k1, psso, k17(18:19), k2tog, k3. 72(76:80) sts.
56th to 62nd rows: Work 7 rows as set.
63rd dec row: K3, sl 1, k1, psso, k15(16:17), k2tog, k28(30:32), sl 1, k1, psso, k15(16:17), k2tog, k3. 68(72:76) sts.
Cont in st st until work measures 34cm/13¼in from beg, ending with a p row. 5 rows
Next inc row: K3, m1, k to last 3 sts, m1, k3. 70(74:78) sts.
Work 5 rows in st st.
Rep the last 6 rows, 4 times more, then work the inc row again. 80(84:88) sts.
Cont in st st until work measures 50cm/19¾in from beg, ending with a p row.

Shape armholes

Cast off 4 sts at beg of next 2 rows.
Dec 1 st each end of the next row and the 3(4:5) foll alt rows. 64(66:68) sts.
Cont in st st until work measures 72(73:74)cm/28½(28¾:29) from beg, ending with a p row.

Shape shoulders

Cast off 9 sts at beg of next 4 rows.
Cast off rem 28(30:32) sts.

LEFT FRONT

Work as right half back to **.
48th to 54th rows: Work 7 rows as set.

55th row: K3, sl 1, k1, psso, k17(18:19), k2tog, k12(13:14), mst 4. 38(40:42) sts.

56th to 62nd rows: Work 7 rows as set.

63rd dec row: K3, sl 1, k1, psso, k15(16:17), k2tog, k12(13:14), m st 4(36:38:40) sts

Cont as set until work measures 34cm/13¼in from beg, ending with a p row.

Next inc row: K3, m1, work to end.

**** Work 5 rows as set. 37(39:41) sts.

Rep the last 6 rows, 4 times more, then work the inc row again. 42(44:46) sts.

Cont as set until work measures 50cm/19¾in from beg, ending at side edge.

Shape armhole

Next row: Cast off 4 sts, work to end.

Patt 1 row – omit this row when working right front.

Dec 1 st at armhole edge on next row and the 3(4:5) foll alt rows. 34(35:36) sts.

Work a further 12 rows – work 13 rows here for right front.

Shape neck

Next row: Patt 4 and leave these sts on a safety-pin, work to end.

Dec 1 st at neck edge on next row and the 11(12:13) foll alt rows. 18 sts.

Cont in st st until work measures the same as back to shoulder shaping, ending at side edge.

Shape shoulder

Cast off 9 sts at beg of next row.

Work 1 row.

Cast off rem 9 sts.

RIGHT FRONT

Mark positions for 6 buttons along left front, placing 1st marker on the 21st row and the remainder evenly spaced, having the last marker 4 rows before neck shaping row.

Work as left half back to ***, but working buttonholes to correspond with markers, working 1st buttonhole on the 21st row thus:

21st buttonhole row: Mst 2, yrn, work 2tog, work to end.

48th to 54th rows: Work 7 rows as set.

55th dec row: Mst 4, k12(13:14), sl 1, k1, psso, k17(18:19), k2tog, k3. 38(40:42) sts.

56th to 62nd rows: Work 7 rows as set.

63rd dec row: Mst 4, k12(13:14), sl 1, k1, psso, k15(16:17), k2tog, k3. 36(38:40) sts.

Cont in st st until work measures 34cm/13¼in from beg ending with a p row.

Next inc row: work to last 3 sts, m1, k3. 37(39:41) sts.

Work as left front from **** to end, noting variations.

SLEEVES

With 4mm (No 8/US 6) needles, cast on 41(43:45) sts.

Mst row: K1, [p1, k1] to end.

Rep last row, 5 times more.

Change to 4½mm (No 7/US 7) needles.

Beg with a k row, work 2 rows in st st.

Inc row: K3, m1, k to last 3 sts, m1, k3. 43(45:47) sts.

Work 7 rows in st st.

Rep last 8 rows, 9 times more, then work the inc row again. 63 (65:67) sts.

Cont in st st until work measures 46cm/18in from beg, ending with a p row.

Shape top

Dec 1 st each end of next row and the 3(4:5) foll alt rows.

Work 1 row.

Cast off rem 55 sts.

RIGHT HALF COLLAR

Join shoulder seams. With wrong side of work facing, using 4mm (No 8/US 6) needles, rejoin yarn to 4 sts on right front safety-pin and mst to end.

***** Keeping continuity of mst, inc 1 st at inner edge of next row and the 15 foll 4th rows. 20 sts.

Mst 1 row – mst 2 rows here for left half collar.

Shape collar

1st and 2nd turning rows: Mst 11, sl 1, turn for 1st row, mst to end for 2nd row.

Mst 4 rows.

Rep last 6 rows until inner edge fits up right front neck to shoulder and across to centre back neck.

Cast off.

LEFT HALF COLLAR

With right side of work facing, using 4mm (No 8/US 6) needles, rejoin yarn to the 4 sts on left front safety-pin and mst 2 rows. Work as right half collar from ***** to end, noting variation.

TO MAKE UP

Set sleeves into armholes. Join side and sleeve seams. Sew shaped edge of collar up neck edge and across to centre back neck, then join seam. Catch the 4 cast-off sts at right half back opening under left half back. Sew on buttons.

Rowan yarn addresses

Rowan Yarns are widely available in yarn shops. For details of stockists and mail order sources of Rowan Yarns, please write to or contact the distributors listed below.

UNITED KINGDOM
Rowan Yarns
Green Lane Mill
Holmfirth
West Yorkshire HD7 1RW
Tel: (01484) 681 881

USA
Westminster Fibers
5 Northern Boulevard
Amherst
NH 03031
Tel: (603) 886 5041/5043

AUSTRALIA
Coats Spencer Crafts
Level 1
382 Wellington Road
Private Bag 15
Mulgave North
Victoria 3170
Tel: (39) 561 2288

BELGIUM
Pavan
Koningin Astridlaan 78
B9000 Gent
Tel: (092) 21 85 94

CANADA
Diamond Yarn
9698 St Laurent
Montreal
Quebec H3L 2NI
Tel: (514) 388 6188

Martin Ross
Unit 3
Toronto
Ontario M3J 2L9
Tel: (416) 736 6111

DENMARK
Ruzicka
Hydesbyvej 27
DK 4990 Saskoing
Tel: (8) 54 70 78 04

FRANCE
Elle Tricote
52 rue Principale
67300 Schiltigheim
Tel: (33) 88 62 65 31

GERMANY
Wolle + Design
Wolfshover Strasse 76
52428 Julich Stetternich
Tel: (49) 2461 54735

HOLLAND
de Afstap
Oude Leliestraat 12
1015 Amsterdam
Tel: (020) 623 1445

HONG KONG
East Unity Company Ltd
RM902
Block A
Kailey Industrial Centre
12 Fung Yip Street
Chai Wan
Tel: (852) 2869 7110

ICELAND
Stockurinn
Kjorgardi
Laugavegi 59
ICE-101 Reykjavik
Tel: (01) 551 82 58

ITALY
Victoriana
Via Fratelli Pioli 14
Rivoli
Torino
Tel: (011) 95 32 142

JAPAN
Diakeito Co Ltd
2-3-11 Senba-Higashi
Minoh City
Osaka 562
Tel: (0727) 27 6604

NORWAY
c/o Ruzicka
(see Denmark)

SWEDEN
Wincent
Norrtulsgaten 65
11345 Stockholm
Tel: (08) 673 70 60

Yarn, kits, ready-to-wear garments, books and toys are available from Debbie Bliss's shop:

Debbie Bliss
365 St John Street
London EC1V 4LB
Tel: 020 7833 8255
Fax: 020 7833 3588
web site: www.debbiebliss.freeserve.co.uk

Acknowledgments

This book would not have been possible without the invaluable contribution of the following:

The knitters: Pat Church, Connie Critchell, Janet Fagan, Jacqui Halstead, Shirley Kennett, Maisie Lawrence, Beryl Salter and Frances Wallace.

Penny Hill, who coordinated the knitters and met the deadlines!

The children and models: a big thank you to Nell, Billy, Titus, Emma, Cabral, Lucy, Scarlett, Marcie, Harry, Hannah and Kayleigh and Lauren.

Craig Fordham, the photographer, and Jemima Mills, the stylist, who not only evoked perfectly the spirit of the book but also created a harmonious and inspirational atmosphere to work in.

Emma Callery, whose support and professionalism during the project was invaluable.

Ciara Lunn, whose organisational skills were accompanied by calmness and good humour.

Denise Bates, my editor, who initiated and inspired the project.

Heather Jeeves, my agent, for her total command of contracts!

In addition, the publisher would like to thank the following people and companies who lent clothes for the photographs:

Cath Kidston, 8 Clarendon Cross, London W11 4AP. Tel: 020 7221 4000 (vintage 30s-50s fabrics, clothes and furnishings)
O.B. Trading. Tel: 020 7731 3693 for appointment (vintage clothes)
Boden. Tel: 020 8453 1345 for catalogue (mail order clothing)

Photographed on location at Garth Gell Farmhouse in Wales. Available to rent as holiday cottage. Call Johnny Holland on 0976 368179 for details.